MAKING OF THE
IIT BRAND

RECOUNTING THE JOURNEY OF IIT'S ALUMNI AND ITS GROWTH TO FAME

TRIALS AND MEMORIES OF AN INSTITUTION

DAVENDER JAIN

INDIA • SINGAPORE • MALAYSIA

Contents

Foreword

Today, the Indian Institute of Technology (IIT) consistently ranks among the world's top universities and is a cradle of some of India's best technical minds.

Back in the 1950s, the academic, research and leadership excellence of the IIT system remarkably drove the engine that powered the future of independent India.

IIT Kharagpur, the first institute in the IIT umbrella, was set up in 1950, when the nation was wrestling with colossal challenges. Independence had come at a time when the world was beginning to rebuild itself after a devastating war. India too had many difficulties to overcome, not the least being dire poverty, the ravages of Partition, and the absence of national self-belief after centuries of colonial rule.

The need was never greater for institutions of excellence that could set the tone for socio-economic progress, industrial development, food and social security, defence and overall national growth.

So, it is only fitting that IIT Kharagpur started its life with a patriotic fire in its belly. It was first housed in Hijli Detention Camp in Kharagpur, West Bengal, a British prison that used to hold political prisoners and freedom fighters. In 1951, as India planned its first world-class engineering and technology institute, Prime Minister Jawaharlal Nehru chose Hijli as its site on the advice of the then West Bengal Chief Minister, Bidhan Chandra Roy.

IIT Kharagpur would thus be sanctified by the many sacrifices of the freedom fighters representing the aspirations of the Indian people.

At IIT Kharagpur's first convocation in 1956, Prime Minister Nehru said, "Here in the place of that Hijli Detention Camp stands the fine monument of India, representing India's urges, India's future in the making. This picture seems to me symbolical of the changes that are coming to India."

Clearly, India's leaders had an expansive and bold vision for what the IITs would accomplish. They set the bar really high right from the start, aiming to develop the IITs to be on par with the Massachusetts Institute of Technology in the US. The initial plan was to establish IITs across the nation without regional imbalance, in the east, west, north and south— in Kharagpur, Bombay, Kanpur, Delhi and Madras to be precise. There are 22 IITs today.

Over 70 years have passed since IIT Kharagpur opened its doors as the first IIT. This book is an attempt to present the achievements of this institution of excellence, reflecting on the journeys of several generations of IITians that the individual institutes moulded over the years.

This book collates the stories told by the IITians themselves. They share their dreams, the challenges they overcame, and some of their contributions to society, built on the firm foundations that IIT provided. Together they gave IITs the brand name IIT that attracts multinationals from overseas in hordes to recruit at salaries competitive with Harvard and MIT of USA.

The book does not seek to glorify particular IITians and their achievements. Instead, it focuses on telling the stories of human interest— from the first graduating class of 1955 till the early 1970s. The book recounts the stories of alumni who have played no small role in giving IIT its brand name. Through these stories, you will see the difference these IITians have made, not only for India but also for the entire world.

The book will hopefully be a historical record of the IITs and their alumni. The book also aims to inspire generations of youngsters, particularly students and IIT aspirants, who will continue to build on the tradition of excellence that the IITs stand for.

O P Khanna
1957-61, Mechanical, Patel Hall
Chairman, Needy Heart Foundation, Bengaluru
Formerly with UN in Uganda
Former Executive Director and Managing Director of a large German-Swiss multinational

The Indian Institute of Technology (IIT): A Glimpse

The Indian Institute of Technology Kharagpur was the first IIT founded in 1951 by India's first Prime Minister, Pandit Jawaharlal Nehru (1947-64). At his behest, under the auspices of the United Nations Educational, Scientific and Cultural Organization (UNESCO), the Massachusetts Institute of Technology (MIT) stepped forward to head a consortium of 13 international universities, which also included the University of Manchester in England, to help establish the first IIT in Kharagpur, India.

Classes began in August 1951 in an old building located on a campus of 1800 acres, donated by the Government of West Bengal, in Hijli, 5 kilometres south of Kharagpur. This building had served as a military/air force base during World War II. In the first class, there were just 42 teachers and 224 students, with 10 departments.

Then Pandit Nehru laid the foundation stone in March 1952 for a new handsome building, with a majestic tower, designed by the eminent Swiss architect, Dr. M. Moser. It began functioning in 1955. On September 15, 1956, the Parliament of India passed the Indian Institute of Technology (Kharagpur) Act, declaring it an 'Institute of National Importance'. At the inaugural convocation of IIT Kharagpur in 1956, Prime Minister Nehru presided over the conferring of the first-ever IIT-engineering degrees upon the graduating class of 1955. In that class was Jogendra Singh, the future founder of the Indian Institute of Technology Kharagpur Alumni Association.

For the first seven years, there was only one IIT, until IIT Bombay was founded in 1958, with assistance from Russia (then part of the USSR). Later came IIT Madras in 1959 (with German assistance), IIT Kanpur in 1960 (with American assistance) and IIT Delhi in 1961 (with British assistance). They all used the template provided by IIT Kharagpur, under the guidance of the distinguished 22-member N. R. Sarkar Committee. They were all directly funded by the University Grants Commission (UGC), an agency of the Government of India.

The IITs receive comparatively higher grants than other engineering colleges in India. They are still approximately 80% subsidised by the Ministry of Human Resources and Development (MHRD), which has replaced the UGC. The remaining 20% is made up of student fees, research funding from the industry and contributions from the alumni. The IITs have a relatively high faculty-to-student ratio of 1:6 to 1:8, which makes for an exceptionally strong teacher-student bond and greater contact time. This ratio, even when compared to the very best universities in the world, such as Harvard, Oxford, MIT, Cambridge and Caltech, is exceptionally high and probably accounts for the strength and excellence of IIT graduates, along with the fact that all student selection is done only through the Joint Entrance Exam (JEE).

Recently, student selection was split into two parts. Students must first pass 'JEE-Main' to be able to sit for 'JEE Advanced', from which the final cut is made. In the case of M. Tech and PhD, students also have to pass the Graduate Aptitude Test in Engineering (GATE), before they are admitted to graduate programmes.

As per the Thacker Committee Report of 1959-61, all M. Tech students and research scholars are provided with scholarships. The medium of instruction in all IITs is English. The electronic library in each IIT allows students to access online journals and periodicals. There are also free online videos of actual lectures in different disciplines under the National Programme on Technology Enhanced Learning (NPTEL). This initiative has been undertaken to make quality education accessible to all students.

The IITs soon established themselves as India's premier educational institutions, providing engineers and other applied scientists to manage India's budding industrial sectors, such as steel, fertilisers and chemicals, aerospace, shipbuilding, electronics, computers, information technology, biotechnology, nanotechnology and telecommunications.

The IITs quickly attained international recognition for the excellence of their graduates, many of whom sought higher degrees in the USA, the UK, Canada, Germany, Australia, Russia, Japan and now even China. For the year 2006, the *Times* of London, UK, in its *Higher Educational Supplement*, ranked the then 7 IITs (which by now included IIT Guwahati and IIT Roorkee) grouped together as a single entity as #3 in the world in technology, just after MIT (#1) and Berkeley (#2), ahead of Stanford University (#4). Since then, the *Times* has been ranking the IITs separately; unfortunately, the IITs no longer rank very high individually. Their main shortcoming is in the area of research, which requires a great deal of funding, which the Indian government/industry/alumni cannot provide as yet.

Around 2007, the American TV Network, CBS, in its documentary *60 Minutes,* did a segment on IIT. The veteran correspondent Leslie Stahl said, "If you were to put Harvard, MIT and Princeton together, you would begin to get an idea of the status of this school in India." On July 22, 2011, Canada's national newspaper, *The Globe and Mail,* reported in an article titled 'Folio, Making the Grade' (Pgs. A 8-9): "The IITs are 16 separate engineering colleges spread across India which, taken together, are perhaps the most elite educational institutions in the world. More than 500,000 students wrote the entrance exam this year. Just 8,000 were admitted. This is an acceptance ratio of less than 2%, lower than that of, for example, Harvard University or Oxford. An IIT degree is a passport to wealth and respect."

A complete listing of all the newer autonomous IITs, with a write-up on each, is provided in the last chapter of this book.

Chapter 1

The Pioneers

Satish Aggarwal

Satish Aggarwal had a humble start with a merit-cum-means scholarship at IIT Kharagpur. He started off as an employee at Mahindra and Mahindra and later became the owner of a small winery outlet left behind by his father in 1974. He expanded it to scores of wine shops and depots all over Andhra Pradesh and Telangana. In the early 80s, he became the owner of a prominent distillery and brewery in India. There was no stopping him. He also established steel and chemical factories and a spinning mill in the early 90s. He left behind the Kumar Group of Industries, whose chairman he was before he died in 2017. Read his story to learn how he did it all. It is one of the most fascinating stories you will ever read.

Professor (Dr) Prem Vrat

Prem Vrat was born in a village near Delhi in an economically weak family. He was the son of a marginal farmer. His parents had no formal education, though they were intelligent, value-driven and hardworking. Getting into teaching and research at IIT Delhi in 1968 had a transformational effect on his life and career. Prem still continues to teach at IIT Delhi; this is his 54th year of teaching. He was also a professor of eminence at MDI, Gurugram. Prem was a vice-chancellor at ITM University. The university was rechristened 'The NorthCap University, Gurugram', where Prem continues to work as the pro-chancellor.

As the director of IIT Roorkee in 2001, Prem played a key facilitating role in the transformation of the erstwhile University of Roorkee into IIT Roorkee. His story is another amazing story of giving back to the IIT system in return for what IIT Kharagpur gave him.

Arjun Menda

Arjun Menda was born in 1933 in a place called Shikarpur in Sindh, which is now in Pakistan. When Partition took place, his family had to flee, leaving behind everything they had built over generations. When Arjun wanted to study engineering, it was clearly beyond the family's means. Seeing their hardships, a kind gentleman offered Arjun Rs 11 as a refugee scholarship to study. Now Arjun is one of the biggest developers/builders in India.

Over the last 25 years, Arjun has funded over 20,000 students with scholarships and provided e-learning kits to more than 2,000 schools in Karnataka. His foundation has also set up solar stations at homes and student hostels, benefitting over three lakh students.

Kalyan Banerjee

Kalyan Banerjee is the director of United Phosphorus Ltd, the largest agro-chemical manufacturer in India. He invented the red phosphorous used in matchsticks. Kalyan became the president of Rotary International in 2011, leading 1.2 million Rotarians in over 200 countries. He is only the third Indian ever to occupy this job in the 100+ years of Rotary International's history. He also led the Rotary Foundation during its centennial year in 2016-17 and raised over $300 million towards service projects worldwide.

Madhusudan Chakraborty

Madhusudan Chakraborty gave up a lucrative career in the auto industry to join IIT Kharagpur as a lecturer of materials science in 1974. The freedom to pursue his passion made him linger on in the lush green campus for 50 years, including his years as a student. While teaching the bright students of IIT was satisfying and enriching, the major challenge for him was to overcome the roadblocks in the realm of experimental research. His struggle paid rich dividends in the form of collaboration with industry giants like TELCO Jamshedpur and R&D laboratories like DMRL Hyderabad and sponsored projects from CSIR, DST and DRDO. Extramural support helped in creating research facilities not only for his group but also for other researchers.

Other than teaching and research, Madhusudan was roped in by the institute to shoulder many administrative responsibilities such as chairmanship of Central Research Facility, heading metallurgical and materials engineering, and being the dean of postgraduate studies and research, the dean of alumni affairs and internal relations, and the deputy director during 1991-2009.

The most exciting challenge in his career, prior to retirement, was the setting up of an IIT in Bhubaneswar during 2009-2014. With deep satisfaction, Madhusudan finally bade goodbye to the campus in 2016.

Against All Odds

Late Satish Kumar Aggarwal

1964-1969, B. Tech - Metallurgy, Nehru Hall, IIT Kharagpur

Satish Kumar had a humble start with a merit-cum-means scholarship at IIT Kharagpur. He started off as an employee at Mahindra and Mahindra and later became the owner of a small winery outlet left behind by his father in 1974. He expanded it to scores of wine shops and depots all over Andhra Pradesh and Telangana. In the early 80s, he became the owner of a prominent distillery and brewery in India. There was no stopping him. He also established steel and chemical factories and a spinning mill in the early 90s. He left behind the Kumar Group of Industries, whose chairman he was before he died in 2017.

As shared by Davender Jain

Satish joined a close-knit group of four when he joined Cambridge school in Delhi. The five of us became good friends.

In 1964, four of us took the IIT exam and chose IIT Kharagpur as our college and Nehru Hall as our hall of residence. We didn't know that Satish's father had refused to support his higher education because of financial hardships. One day, as we were sitting at the terrace in Nehru Hall, drinking tea, we saw Satish entering the hall in old clothes. This was unlike him. We then discovered that he was on a merit-cum-means scholarship.

During the college days, Satish used to persuade us to go to movies in Kharagpur town, particularly when the exams were on. He was like Aamir Khan in the movie *3 Idiots—beheti hawa sa tha woh.* In 1969, he won the Nehru Cup at IIT, which is given to the distinguished outgoing student.

On passing out in 1969, we realised that there were no jobs as multinationals had been kicked out by Mrs Indira Gandhi and the few private sector companies in the country paid as poorly as the public sector firms. Some of us went to the US to do an MS and others joined their family business. Satish joined his uncle's shoe factory in Chandigarh, only to find out that he was ill-suited for the job. He quit and applied to the newly established IIM Ahmedabad and got selected. His father came down heavily on him, refusing to support his education any further. His parents had to support and bring up two of his sisters and three of his brothers, who were all younger to Satish. But Satish was a strong person. On passing out from IIT Kharagpur and IIM-A on merit scholarship, his life changed.

Satish landed a good job with Mahindra and Mahindra (tractor division) and took a posting in Hyderabad, where his father was running a small wine shop. Satish did two jobs—helping his father run the wine shop in the evening and at night and a day job with Mahindra and Mahindra. His father died unexpectedly in 1974, leaving behind one married daughter, one unmarried daughter, three unmarried sons, a widowed mother, and a dependent wife. Satish had no option but to quit his job and run the wine shop full-time. He was only 27 years old then.

Against all odds, Satish expanded his wine shop business with the support of his well-wishers. Within a span of just five years, he had more than ten wine shops, a few godowns, and the distributorship of branded liquor and beer in Andhra Pradesh and Maharashtra. Learning from his experience from Mahindra and Mahindra, Satish opened a tractor showroom in the name of 'International Tractors' in the late 70s and supplied branded tractors all over Andhra Pradesh.

There was a brewery in Hyderabad owned by the Jains of Delhi. Between 1980 and 1982, Satish sold so much of their beer that one day he was called by the marketing director for lunch. The marketing director was so impressed by him that he recommended Satish to be taken on board of the brewery. Once he was on the board, Satish impressed the Jains and became their friend.

The brewery was ageing and the Jains in Bombay had no intentions of investing in it to refurbish it. Satish saw an opportunity here. He made an offer to the Jains—he would pay a reasonable down payment to them for the purchase of the factory and the remaining amount would be paid from the earnings of the factory, which would be run under his management and control. Trusting his competence, the Jains agreed to the offer. Within one year, Satish paid the balance consideration to the Jains and became the complete owner of the factory and the company.

Satish worked day and night, often sleeping in the brewery itself. He refurbished it and repaired the equipment and machinery. As beer was a popular drink in Hyderabad, Satish struck gold with the brewery. Considering his growth and popularity in the liquor industry in the state of Andhra Pradesh, he was made the chairman of a steering committee—an association of all the manufacturers and wholesale and retail dealers of liquor and beer in Andhra Pradesh.

Under his chairmanship, the association became stronger and all the wholesale and retail dealers felt safe and secure to do business. He was the voice and face of the liquor industry in front of government departments and other authorities. Under his chairmanship, the liquor association mobilised millions of rupees as donation for the cyclone relief fund in 1990 and handed over a cheque to the then chief minister of Andhra Pradesh, Mr M. Chenna Reddy. Due to this generous gesture by the liquor association, many other associations representing other businesses came forward and donated to the cyclone relief fund.

In the early 90s, considering his business turnover, income and experience, Satish built a few more factories, namely a steel plant, a chemical plant and a spinning mill. All his companies gave employment to hundreds of skilled and unskilled workers and professionals. Several ancillary units came up near his factories, providing direct income and employment to hundreds of people.

Satish and his group of companies worked on putting up a port and a power plant at Vijinjham in Kerala. They got a letter of intent from the government in 1995. Satish personally signed an MoU with the ports secretary, Government of Kerala, in the presence of the then Chief Minister of Kerala, Mr K. Karunakaran.

In 1995, Satish was invited to be part of a delegation of prospering businessmen from India to attend a business seminar in Malaysia, headed by the then Prime Minister of India, Mr P.V. Narasimha Rao.

In the mid-90s, Satish became one of the founding members of IIM Ahmedabad Alumni Association – Hyderabad chapter and worked towards spreading the popularity of the association. The association raised millions of rupees every year and donated the same for social causes. It organised different kinds of social camps, worked on providing education to poor children, conducted business seminars for networking, and worked for the growth of graduates, entrepreneurs and professionals.

Unfortunately, Satish's elder son, who was only 20 years old, passed away in 1997 in an accident. This shattered Satish and his family, and he stopped working on business expansion. His businesses went through different cycles of national recession and changing government policies from time to time.

Satish suffered from medical problems since 2010 and was on peritoneal dialysis for more than seven years. He lost more than half of his eyesight between 2015 and 2017. He fractured his leg in 2016 and was wheelchair-bound for nearly two years till he expired in November 2017. But, in the last seven years of his life, in spite of adverse medical conditions, he fought against all odds. He went to office regularly, attended social events, and continued working till he breathed his last. According to his family members, all this was possible for him because of his optimistic way of looking at things, his strong mind, his determination, and his never-give-up attitude, as a result of his tough experiences in life.

This is a story of an IITian who was no less than Aamir Khan from the movie *3 Idiots*. If I was asked to describe Satish in one sentence, I would say, "A man with a big heart who was always optimistic in life."

Lastly, I would like to add this, *"Woh kahan gaya usey dhoondo."* (Where has he gone? Search for him.)

Throughout his life, Satish worked smart and hard. Eventually, he left with happy memories. He is a great inspiration for his family and all his well-wishers.

I believe his life is a learning lesson as well as an inspiration for all IITians.

The remarkable story of Satish Kumar Aggarwal has been shared by his friend Davender Jain.

My Tale to Tell: The Challenges of Setting up an IIT

Professor (Dr) Prem Vrat

1962-1966, B. Tech (Hons) - Mechanical Engineering, RP Hall, IIT Kharagpur

Prem Vrat was born in a village near Delhi in an economically weak family. He was the son of a marginal farmer. His parents had no formal education, though they were intelligent, value-driven and hardworking. Getting into teaching and research at IIT Delhi in 1968 had a transformational effect on his life and career. Prem still continues to teach at IIT Delhi; this is his 54th year of teaching. He is also a professor of eminence at MDI, Gurugram. Prem was a vice-chancellor at ITM University. The university was rechristened 'The NorthCap University, Gurugram', where Prem continues to work as the pro-chancellor.

I joined IIT Kharagpur in 1962 in the four-year B. Tech (honours) programme in mechanical engineering and graduated in 1966. I did M. Tech in industrial engineering and operations research from the same institute in 1968. I was the resident of R. P. Hall of Residence during both my UG and PG. My life was transformed by my alma mater, IIT Kharagpur, which I normally call as the mother of the IIT system, being the eldest and the largest in the system.

I joined IIT Delhi on 9th August, 1968 as a lecturer in the mechanical engineering department. I enrolled in a part-time PhD in IIT Delhi and received a PhD in 1974.

Thus, I can say that I have all my degrees from the IIT system and I am a fully homegrown *swadeshi* academic.

IIT Kharagpur honoured me with the Distinguished Alumnus Award in 2004, which was conferred on me during its golden jubilee convocation. IIT Delhi bestowed on me the Distinguished Service Award.

I was born in a village in an economically weak family. I was the son of a marginal farmer. My parents had no formal education, though they were intelligent, value-driven and hardworking.

I studied in a village that had no electricity. I studied under the light of a kerosene lamp.

I was in a Hindi medium school up to 12th standard. I gave my board examination in 12th under the UP board in 1962 in the Hindi medium. I secured distinction in chemistry, physics and mathematics, which entitled me to a national merit scholarship of Rs 110 per month (in 1962, this was a good amount). This enabled me to study at IIT Kharagpur.

The JEE entrance exam was in English. But I was fortunate to get a high JEE rank, which enabled me to get into mechanical engineering at IIT Kharagpur, which was the most sought-after branch in IIT those days. In the first year, I faced some difficulty in studying in the English medium but I could soon catch up. I graduated in B. Tech (honours) and M. Tech with top grades. Life at IIT Kharagpur was great despite some difficulties being a vegetarian.

Teaching and research at IIT Delhi since 1968 has had a transformational effect on my life and career. I still continue to teach here. This is the 54th year of teaching at IIT Delhi.

I have held almost all academic and administrative positions at IIT Delhi— from lecturer, professor and now an honorary professor to head, dean, deputy director and director (officiating).

I was invited to be a professor and division chairman of the industrial engineering and management division of the prestigious Asian Institute of Technology, Bangkok, Thailand (1989-91). Though it was a short stint, because I did not want to leave IIT Delhi and settle in Thailand for long, it was a remarkable journey for me. The courtesy and respect I received from colleagues and students from 25-30 countries was incredible. Even now I feel nostalgic about this stint, like I feel about my student days at IIT Kharagpur.

Then a major role came my way—transforming the really old and reputed technical university, University of Roorkee, into the newest IIT in 2001 (IIT Roorkee). I was appointed the founder director of IIT Roorkee. My role as the first director had enormous challenges and opportunities. And when I look back, I have a sense of great satisfaction that I could inspire and motivate all stakeholders to make the institute a truly top-ranking IIT, which consistently ranked sixth in the IIT system comprising 23 institutes.

I had another challenge when I was invited to become the vice-chancellor of UP Technical University (UPTU) at Lucknow, which had a mandate over all engineering, management, pharmacy and architecture colleges, both government and private, across the entire state of Uttar Pradesh. I played a key role in enhancing the academic excellence of UPTU-affiliated colleges and introduced a compulsory audit course in all the programmes of UPTU on 'human values and professional ethics'. This was a bold initiative back then and I am happy to note that it has now become compulsory in almost all AICTE-affiliated institutions in India.

The second initiative was to develop and implement the UPTU Academic Excellence Award Model with top experts as members of a jury headed by Professor Damodar Acharya, when he was Chairman of AICTE. This led to a healthy competition among colleges focused on total quality.

Later I was invited to be a professor of eminence at MDI, Gurugram and vice-chancellor at ITM University where I still continue as pro-chancellor. ITM University has now a new name—The NorthCap University (NCU), Gurugram.

One common feature across my journey has been that I have always taught classes, guided research, and published papers, irrespective of the many administrative positions I have held at IIT Delhi, IIT Roorkee, UPTU and now at NCU, and even as the pro-chancellor and chairman, Board of Governors (BOG), IIT (ISM) Dhanbad/IIT Mandi.

I still teach at NCU as well as IIT Delhi and guide PhD scholars at both the institutes. I have been an IITian for the past 59 years—from a UG student at IIT Kharagpur in 1962 to honorary professor at IIT Delhi and now the chairman, BOG. Incidentally, I was the first graduate of IIT Kharagpur since its inception to have become a regular director of any IIT in 2001. I am fortunate to be associated with four IITs and I have experienced a long journey, starting from my days as a B. Tech student to being the chairman, Board of Governors, travelling across IIT along the entire chain.

When I look back on this long journey of more than 59 years in the IIT system, I have a sense of satisfaction. I have supervised 47 PhD theses (3 more are in the advanced stage), 118 M. Tech dissertations, and 65 B. Tech major projects. I have published 504 research papers in international and national journals and conference proceedings, which have received more than 8400 citations (Google scholar) and interested 1,20,000 readers. One of my papers has received 1650 citations and I have a G-index of 89. I have proposed a simple but comprehensive index (P-index and V-index) for evaluating the quality of research papers and co-authored 7 books, edited 5 conference proceedings, and offered 36 major industrial consultancies.

Fortunately, these efforts have led to reasonably good academic recognitions, honours and awards. Fifteen of my research papers have received the best paper/case study medals and prizes. I was conferred the prestigious fellowships of Indian National Academy of Engineering, National Academy of Sciences, India, World Academy of Productivity Science, Indian Institution of Industrial Engineering, and Indian Society for Technical Education. IIIE conferred upon me the Lillian Gilbreth Award, Life Time Achievement Award and its highest recognition as the Honorary Member. The Systems Society of India conferred on me the Dr. C.M. Jacob Gold Medal for outstanding contributions to systems modelling and management. The IIT Delhi Alumni Association conferred the Outstanding Contribution Award for National Development. Bundelkhand University conferred the Doctor of Engineering (Honoris causa). ISME awarded the Distinguished Mechanical Engineering Educator Award. Other recognitions conferred are Uttaranchal Ratan Award, Centenarian Seva Ratna Award, Guru Award by SAE India Foundation, IES–Dr. J. C. Bose National Excellence Award, Lifetime Achievement Award by Society of Operations Management (SOM), Dr. M. C. Puri Memorial Award of ORSI for outstanding contributions for promotion of operational research in India, and Lifetime Achievement Award by System Society of India and Dayalbagh Educational Institute.

Re-think India conferred the Visionary Edu-leader Award in 2017, which was given to me by the former President of India, Shri Pranab Mukherjee. The Uttar Pradesh Chief Minister, Yogi Adityanath, felicitated me in 2019 for my contributions as the vice-chancellor of UP Technical University, Lucknow. The IEOM Society International (USA) conferred the Distinguished Educator Award on 18th August 2021.

India's Most Visionary EduLeadership Award being conferred on Professor Prem Vrat by the then President of India, Mr Pranob Mukherjee

I have served on the editorial boards of many Indian and international journals. I have been a member of the board of governors of many engineering colleges, member university court in JNU and CUH. I was chairman of INAE Forum on engineering education, chairman of AICTE(NWRC), chairman of National Credit Framework (NCF), and many more. I have delivered many keynote addresses in conferences as well as convocation addresses.

When I look back at my journey–from a humble rural background to all that I have been able to accomplish—I realise that the role of IIT Kharagpur has been tremendous. It has made me what I am today and I offer my grateful thanks to my teachers there who shaped me. I have a strong emotional bond with IIT

Kharagpur and I do hope that my brief profile is able to inspire many in the younger generation who are born in situations similar to mine—that, with sincerity, hard work, honesty and commitment, one can overcome all constraints.

Paying Back the Kindness of Society

Arjun Menda,

1956-1958, M. Tech - Product Technology, IIT Kharagpur

Arjun Menda was born in 1933 in a place called Shikarpur in Sindh, which is now in Pakistan. When Partition took place, his family had to flee, leaving behind everything they had built over generations. When Arjun wanted to study engineering, it was clearly beyond the family's means. Seeing their hardships, a kind gentleman offered Arjun Rs 11 as a refugee scholarship to study. Now Arjun is one of the biggest developers/builders in India.

Over the last 25 years, Arjun has funded over 20,000 students with scholarships and provided e-learning kits to more than 2,000 schools in Karnataka. His foundation has also set up solar stations at homes and student hostels, benefitting over three lakh students.

I was born in 1933 in a place called Shikarpur in Sindh, which is now in Pakistan. When Partition took place, my family had to flee, leaving behind everything we had built over generations. We came to Madras, now called Chennai, where my father had to struggle to make ends meet but he made sure we got good education. But when I wanted to study engineering, it was clearly beyond my family's means. Seeing our hardships, a kind gentleman offered me Rs 11 as a refugee scholarship, so that I could go to Guindy Engineering College in Madras to pursue my pre-engineering and engineering courses.

I had done well enough then to get admitted into a master's programme in production technology at the prestigious IIT Kharagpur.

Then I moved to Bombay, the city everybody now knows as Mumbai, where I started my career as an industrial engineer at Mahindra and Mahindra Ltd. Then I moved to Gabriel India Ltd, where I was promoted to production manager.

I was doing well, thanks to the generosity of that man who helped me with my fees and education. Thereafter, I started promoting a few small-scale industries specialising in the manufacturing of precision tuned parts and pressed parts.

Real estate became a true part of my life only in 1980, when I began constructing residential and commercial buildings. I used my qualifications and expertise to do the best I could in order to make an impact. RMZ Corp was born in Bangalore in 2002. It fills my heart with a lot of pride to see the direction it is moving in, with my sons Raj and Manoj carrying my vision forward. A near-zero debt status and 45 million square feet of leasable office space is no mean feat!

Over the decades, my work has been recognised, which, of course, gives me great joy. My proudest moments came when I was awarded the Lifetime Achievement Award by the Confederation of Real Estate Developers Association of India, in 2017, and the Outstanding Alumni of the Year Award by Indian Institute of Technology Kharagpur, in 2021. I wanted to make sure that I paid back for all the kindness I had received from society, which had brought me to a beautiful point in life.

What gives me the biggest joy is the work we have been doing at the Menda Foundation, which I set up in 1995, to help educate those children and adults whose families couldn't afford education—just like I was helped when my family couldn't. Over the last 25 years, we have funded over 20,000 students with scholarships and provided e-learning kits to more than 2,000 schools in Karnataka. We have also set up solar stations at homes and student hostels, benefitting over 3 lakh students.

Paying back to society in this way has given me great satisfaction.

45 million square feet of leasable office space of RMZ Construction

My Life of Service above the Self

Kalyan Banerjee

1964-1969, B. Tech - Chemical Engineering, Patel Hall, IIT Kharagpur

> *Kalyan Banerjee is the director of United Phosphorus Ltd, the largest agro-chemical manufacturer in India. He invented the red phosphorous used in matchsticks. Kalyan became the president of Rotary International in 2011, leading 1.2 million Rotarians in over 200 countries. He is only the third Indian ever to occupy this job in the 100+ years of Rotary International's history. He also led the Rotary Foundation during its centennial year in 2016-17 and raised over $300 million towards service projects worldwide.*

I started schooling at the age of six, at Tagore's Shanti Niketan, and then spent six years in the splendour of the historic Gwalior Fort, at Scindia School. Later I landed at home in Kolkata in early 1960, wondering what next. My father took me to St Xavier's College for admission, but since I had secured a second class in my ISC exam, the French missionary admission in-charge there said a straightforward "no" to us.

I told my father the next day, "Let me try again alone." I met the same father again and told him that I had stood first in India in my Senior Cambridge exam but had been sick and bedridden during the ISC exam. He said, "Okay, I'll take you in, but I'm going to keep a watch on you to see how good you are."

The next year, at the suggestion of friends who were all doing likewise, I sat for the IIT entrance exam and then waited in hope. Six weeks later, the call for the interview came, on the first day that they called the hopefuls. I may have stood in the 97th place and I told the interview panel that I was seeking to be an architect. They said architecture admissions were not open. Mechanical engineering was already full. I could have chemical engineering or else wait. Well, I did not want to take any chances. So I agreed and landed in Kharagpur in early July. I met a few other freshers hanging around and we thought it was safer to be together.

I don't know why, but the first hall of residence we saw was Patel, supposedly the oldest and nicest (the others never agreed) and we moved in here for accommodation. The only place we got was in the B block, on the ground floor, but as they say beggars can't be choosers. So, we settled in here.

So, Suresh Chawla and Rajesh Dayal from Delhi, Kalyan (that's me) from Kolkata and Alok Mittal from Lucknow grouped together to face the ragging of seniors. Well, nothing worse than cohabiting with three others, or parading in the open and in the rains, bare-bodied with just the underwear, happened.

The next four years passed well for me, in a class of about 36. I learnt some engineering, though I confess I did not study much. SKAR (the four of us) went twice a week to the Railway Institute in town to see English movies. Kharagpur did not have too many women those days and the few women who were present were well attended to. The mess food could not be had for over three continuous days. So, SKAR would go down twice a week to Jimmy's Shack, which was run from Jimmy's house, two miles from the campus where pork, chicken and mutton were served. His food did not cost much and we took turns to feed the four of us, but sometimes scarcity of funds would keep us starving.

In early 1964, I passed out with first-class honours. I stood sixth in class and was congratulated by the principal, Dr. M. N. Rao. My other notable successes in IIT were winning the open tennis doubles one year and an inter-house quiz competition run by the US Embassy in Kolkata.

I started looking for a cushy job at a multinational. Then an uncle, who was working with an MNC, guided me to join a smaller chemical company, which was making rare and hazardous products in indigenous units with a lot of ingenuity. My first three years there was a huge learning experience before I was sent to Assam to start a chemical plant for somebody there. Staying away from floods, snakes and scorpions was a challenge.

After four months in Assam, I went for a medical checkup at Kolkata Medical College. On my fourth day there, the young lady nursing me there, Binota, attracted my attention. So, I contrived to stay there for 45 days, inventing illnesses. When I reluctantly left, Binota agreed to meet me outside. And six months later, we got married. I got thrown out of my home over the issue of caste and background. So, Binota and I migrated to Mumbai.

We had a lot of support from the wonderful Shroff family, who helped us settle down and get going. Six months later, when the Shroffs were opening a new unit in Vapi, South Gujarat, they invited us to join them. And I spent the next 51 years of my life at Vapi, making red phosphorus (used in matches for the first time in India), having two children (they are both married and settled abroad), building a 200-bed hospital, building schools and pharmaceutical colleges, doing an MBA, and taking care of Rotary business, which I had enjoyed from the beginning.

Rising through the Rotary ranks with time, I became its international president in 2011, the third Indian ever to occupy the job to lead 1.2 million Rotarians in over 200 countries. Binota loved Rotary and accompanied me, as I travelled and met people in about 110 countries. In 2012, as president of Rotary International, I was proud to help India become polio-free for the first time ever. Of course, WHO, Bill Gates and the Indian government had worked hard to achieve this but Rotary was most applauded for the achievement.

Unfortunately, Binota started having kidney troubles from 2000. She had a transplant in 2009 and travelled worldwide with me. Then she needed a second transplant, which came from a family member. But she was never quite the same after this and kept going down. I dedicated my time and energy to her and, in late July of 2020, I returned her to the Almighty. Today, at the age of 78, I live in Vapi, helping our hospital grow. I keep trying to do all that I can to educate the Adivasi families living around South Gujarat.

Working to eradicate polio from India was a challenge I had decided to work on. India was considered the toughest place to do this, because of poverty, disease prevalence and primitive village conditions. On January 1, 2011, six months before my rotary presidency started, I visited some remote villages in UP, near Moradabad, which had the most polio cases. In one place with mainly Muslim villagers, I found their tube well located just next to the toilet—a hole in the ground sheltered all around by gunny bags. We got them to shift the toilet further away and told their neighbours to do the same. This simple step, I hoped, would help us solve some of their polio problems.

I followed up with several trips to villages in Bihar, which were often roadless and with problems of floods, jungles, tigers and bandits. Accompanied by two locals, I went to remote villages, traversing rocky terrain through forests. The locals told me we had to return well before dusk, lest tigers met us on the way. In another place in Bihar, we had to cross a swift-flowing river, which had no bridge. So, I got into the regular ferry boat there and was told that there were a few crocodiles in the river. We crossed and went to the village on the other side, knocked on doors that were opened reluctantly, and vaccinated the children after bribing them with sweets.

In the Muslim areas in Makegsin in Maharashtra, near Mumbai, people said that vaccines would make men impotent. I went there with two others, invited the *maulvis* to the mosque, and met them outside. I explained to them that many Muslims in UP and other places had understood the need and safety of vaccine and got themselves and their children protected. Eventually, but slowly, the Muslims here agreed to go ahead with the vaccination.

The two countries that still had polio were Afghanistan and Pakistan. So, I met the Pakistan President, Zardato, in Islamabad and requested him to get the children immunised. He said that he had no problem but asked us Rotarians to meet the Opposition leader. We phoned the Opposition leader and he agreed to meet us at his home after 10 pm when he would be free.

When we met the Opposition leader, he asked me why we wanted save their children when the Americans were bombing them with drones. We responded, "Sir, our plea is to simply immunise to save your children so they are never crippled." He finally agreed, by 1 am, to our request to proceed with immunisation. Pakistan is now on the verge of being polio-free.

Another important event was my meeting with the Afghan President, Hamid Karzai, in Kabul. The US Army in Afghanistan was contacted to help out with the visit. On arrival, an Afghan Rotarian took me to a spartan hostel run by an international NGO. The idea was to avoid international hotels, which were often attacked. Even the hostel was not completely safe and could be attacked any time. I was advised to stay indoors if I did not want to get shot. The next morning, accompanied by armoured US Army vehicles, both in the front and the rear, we Rotarians went to meet the president. We drove through empty streets, with closed houses and windows and gunmen on the roof to handle any Taliban attack. After four more security checks, we entered the presidential residence where President Karzai greeted me with a warm handshake and said, "Welcome, Mr President." He said Rotary's help was important to remove polio and asked us what he could do.

I went to the health minister next, who asked us to make a storage godown for vaccines. This beautiful ministry building was bombed two months later. I may also add that my visit to Kabul was kept a secret because of Taliban issues, and my wife was advised to be at home in India until I returned home safe.

Every Rotary International president organises an annual convention, attended by Rotarians and their families. Mine was in Bangkok where 35,000 people gathered. The Thai King, Bhumibol, was unwell, and so his daughter was to open the event. The Thais said I had to greet her on my knees, but Rotary said an RI President was as important. A small crisis was avoided with the convention chair greeting her in the traditional manner.

Visiting 110 countries, swimming in the Dead Sea, eating all kinds of food, including raw eel and mashed raw meat made into a paste, were some of the adventures we had to go through.

One of my visits to Kathmandu exposed me to two earthquakes. I had to jump down through a window to stay safe at night, so that Rotary could help build over 85 new schools.

Rotary International President, Kalyan Banerjee (centre), presenting the Guinness World Record certificate for blood donation to the District Governor, Ananth H.R. On the right is Rotarian Shekhar Mehta, the current president and the fourth Indian to become the president of Rotary International.

50 Years at IIT Kharagpur

Madhusudan Chakraborty

1966-71, B. Tech - Metallurgy, Gokhale Hall, IIT Kharagpur

Madhusudan Chakraborty gave up a lucrative career in the auto industry to join IIT Kharagpur as a lecturer of materials science in 1974. The freedom to pursue his passion made him linger on in the lush green campus for 50 years, including his years as a student. Other than teaching and research, he was roped in by the institute to shoulder many administrative responsibilities such as the chairmanship of Central Research Facility, heading metallurgical and materials engineering, and being the dean of postgraduate studies and research, the dean of alumni affairs and internal relations, and the deputy director during 1991-2009. The most exciting challenge in his career, prior to retirement, was the setting up of an IIT in Bhubaneswar during 2009-2014. With deep satisfaction, he finally bade goodbye to the campus in 2016.

I had to make a difficult decision. Abandoning a bright career in an industry, foregoing a lucrative pay and ignoring the lure of training in a giant auto manufacturer in the USA was not easy. However, my passion for teaching and research and the unconditional support of my family were forces strong enough for me to overcome my hesitation. I came back to IIT Kharagpur in September 1974 as a lecturer of materials science. The 2100 acres of lush green campus (the erstwhile detention camp for freedom fighters) attracted many eminent academicians from across the globe, who had decided to linger on in the temple of higher learning for nearly a lifetime. The magnetic pull of the campus, the academic freedom and the opportunity to work with stalwarts were additional attractions that made me decide to join the teaching profession. I never had to look back since then. Fifty years of my eventful life (1966-2016) in IIT Kharagpur, including my student days, seemed to have passed very quickly.

The decision of my family regarding my joining the undergraduate programme at IIT Kharagpur was not without a rider. Coming from a family that was uprooted by the Partition of India, the IIT dream was a difficult proposition. Continuation of financial support for five years, the scholarship in particular, was subject to me obtaining a first class in every examination. So, academics should have been my sole concern. Yet I found myself handling thankless jobs in the hall of residence right from day one. The major challenge was to perform on both fronts. Eventually, I did come out with success and, in the process, I learnt how to deliver. Failure did not deter me and my confidence was never shaken.

IIT Kharagpur certainly laid the foundation of what I am today. Teaching the brilliant students of IIT Kharagpur was certainly a pleasant experience. But I faced a huge roadblock as I began my journey in the realm of research. I was an experimentalist by training. Experiments need basic equipment, instruments, materials, uninterrupted power supply and assistants. Many of my senior professors discouraged me from continuing in the teaching profession not only for the poor compensation but also for the not-so-promising future, given that I was a favourite student of them. Fortunately for me, I never regretted my decision.

My love for academy-industry collaboration drove me to continue my research in areas related to my brief industrial exposure. To carry forward my research initiatives, I decided to approach Mr Sarosh J. Ghandy, the then Deputy General Manager (administration) of TELCO Jamshedpur, for help. I knew that he was the most influential person in the company and would certainly extend his helping hand, if convinced. A warm Mr Ghandy surprised me with his quick and judicious decisions. He sent a huge quantity of materials to IIT Kharagpur for my research work. In addition, he provided me access to the laboratory and testing facilities of the company unconditionally and treated me like a company guest to take care of my accommodation and food during my visits to Jamshedpur. His colleague, Dr. P. S. Pattihal, who mentored me (along with Professor Brij K Dhindaw) for my dissertation for the master's programme, continued to work with me. Mr Ghandy kept enquiring about the progress of my work every time we met.

In addition to my ongoing research, I decided to venture into an unchartered territory to keep me afloat in the academic arena. My collaboration with Defence Metallurgical Research Laboratory (DMRL) Hyderabad opened up new avenues for me. I began to work on aluminium-lithium alloys for space application with DMRL Hyderabad, which had all the experimental facilities one could ask for, and such work could not have been carried out in IIT Kharagpur. Along with my collaborators and students, I continued to work for years on light alloys and metal matrix composites and continued to publish in reputed journals.

I continued to receive research funding from DRDO, DST and CSIR. This helped me create research facilities not only for my group but also for many other researchers. Even funding from the Ministry of Steel, Ministry of Human Resources and Development and an institute were made available to me to create state-of-the-art research facilities.

IIT Kharagpur offered me all the opportunities to satisfy all my passions. Other than teaching and research, I cultivated a passion for administration since my student days. Naturally, I did not hesitate to take up additional responsibilities as and when required.

My association with the Technology Film Society as treasurer and vice-chairman kept me totally occupied. It was fun running the film society that every alumnus loves to talk about. Subsequently, I shouldered many responsibilities—I was the Chairman of Central

Research Facility (1991-96), founder chairman OPTEL-IIT Fibre Optics R&D Centre (1993-96), Dean of Postgraduate Studies and Research (1996-1999), Head of Metallurgical and Materials Engineering (2000-03), Dean of Alumni Affairs and International Relations (2003-06), Founder Chairman of Steel Technology Centre (2008-2009) and Deputy Director (2006-09).

I was the first dean of Alumni Affairs and International Relations probably in the entire IIT system. My experience of running alumni affairs as the secretary of Technology Alumni Association (1976-78) helped me in initiating the work for networking the alumni across the globe. I had to travel extensively to the US, the UK and Singapore and the metros in India to meet the alumni who had been playing an important role in the development of IIT Kharagpur.

Instituting the Distinguished Alumnus Award and the Annual Alumni Meet were some of my initiatives. I also played a catalyst role in the formation of the IIT Kharagpur Alumni Foundation (India). Mr B. K. Syngal, Mr R. S. Mani, Mr Y. P. Suri, Mr Nirmal Bhardwaj, Mr S. M. Murmu, Mr M. Balachandran, Cdr V. K. Jaitley and a few other alumni worked with me tirelessly for the purpose.

I joined IIT Bhubaneswar as its first director on 19th May 2009. The institute began its journey from the campus of IIT Kharagpur in 2008 with about 100 students. The major challenge for me was to commence the academic session in the city of Bhubaneswar from 22nd July 2009. My only support was the registrar who had joined a couple of months ago. A few faculty members were selected by IIT Kharagpur, which was the mentor institute. But they were yet to join. There were about 200 second- and first-year students who had to be taken care of. The available infrastructure for the temporary campus was only the IIT Kharagpur Extension Centre. But that was insufficient for setting up offices, faculty seating rooms, classrooms, laboratories and a workshop. The immediate task ahead was not only to get the institute functioning in the temporary campus by creating the necessary infrastructure but also to arrange accommodation for the students. IIT Kharagpur, the mentor institute, supported by constructing additional buildings in its Extension Centre. IIT Bhubaneswar had to erect a shed with prefabricated materials and renovate a dilapidated building (Toshali Plaza) to accommodate the needs of the temporary campus.

The Government of Odisha allotted about 936 acres of forest land full of cashew trees at Arugul, about a 40-minute drive from the city. The Government of India allocated 76 million Indian rupees. The country and the people of Odisha in particular were looking forward to the news on the development of the new campus. The pressure was heavy and I had to perform. The process of preparation of a master plan, environmental clearance and site development, construction of roads and buildings, and setting up services, such as water supply, electricity, and internet connectivity with adequate bandwidth, were much slower than that I could imagine. The processes of NGT clearance and government spending were painfully slow. Fortunately, support kept pouring in from all corners. The then secretary of higher education, Government of India, and the Chief Minister of Odisha, in particular, kept me on the right track. It was a pleasure driving through the new campus that was almost ready for accommodating the new IIT before my tenure was over.

My tenure at IIT Bhubaneswar ended the year I superannuated and I was back to my home—IIT Kharagpur. I taught for about a year after my retirement and finally decided to bid adieu to the campus in 2016.

Chapter 2

The World: Enter the IITians

Davender Jain

This is a story of hard work and intelligence and how they paid for Davender Jain, particularly when his father's wealthy business empire came to an end, following the rise of ULFA and SULFA terrorists in Assam. This is a little-told story of the family leaving Assam just like how the Kashmir Hindus left Kashmir. Their factories, trucks and other assets were burned down.

The story of Davender Jain is a story of taking risks in life and handling situations and jobs as diverse as they can be—by moving from Assam to the USA, then back to India, then to the World Bank, and then to the UN. After accepting the post of an advisor to work for the Parliament of New South Wales in Sydney, Davender decided to settle down in Australia.

After worldwide travel, Davender finally found Australia the best country to settle down in. His is an amazing story of meeting challenges and hardships, showing perseverance and rebuilding life, after losing everything in Assam.

Ganesh Prasad

Ganesh Prasad grew up in a family of academics. His father was a professor at the prestigious Indian Institute of Science (IISc), Bangalore, and his mother was a school teacher. His childhood was spent in the quiet and green IISc campus, in the company of the children of other professors.

Although he was academically privileged, it took Ganesh several angst-filled years before he finally found his calling. He pursued more than one professional line of study, before giving it up and switching to another. He also learnt several useful life lessons during this journey, sometimes the hard way.

In this story, Ganesh shares his experiences and learnings in the hope that they will be useful and encouraging to younger people on the threshold of their tertiary education or working life. Some of his insights into the positives and negatives of India's elite institutions of learning may be interesting to readers.

Abbas Raza Alvi

Abbas Raza was educated in India, Russia and Australia. He is a poet, a writer, a speaker, a creative community networker and an entrepreneur. He is a strong advocate of protection of the environment and renewable energy.

This is a story of an IITian who joined B. Tech in IIT Kharagpur due to his passion for aeroplanes and then left IIT Kharagpur to go to Russia on a fully-paid Government of India scholarship (including air fares). Then he came back to teach from where he left off. He currently lives in Sydney, Australia.

His credentials

- Hon Life Member of the Australia India Business Council and Founder President of Australia India Chamber of Commerce
- Member of the Art and Multicultural Advisory sub-committees
- Director of Mount Druitt Community Agency
- President of We Australians Are Creative Incorporated
- Former board member of the Ethnic Communities Council of NSW and current president of the Indian Crescent Society of Australia

Abbas promotes multiculturalism, peace and harmony in Australia.

K. Ganga Raju

At the age of 10 years, Ganga Raju used to take cattle for grazing the fields every Sunday. Sometime between 11 am and noon, an aeroplane used to fly over the agricultural fields. Seeing this, Ganga Raju wanted to travel in an aeroplane. That was his childhood dream. His elder brother suggested that he should be good at English and mathematics to make his dream come true. So, Ganga Raju started getting up every day at 4 am to study. As there was no electricity in his small town, he had to study under the light of a hurricane lamp.

In 1966, after B. Sc, he wrote a lateral entrance exam for IIT Bombay and got selected for chemical engineering. However, owing to the financial difficulties of his family, he applied for a Government of India Merit scholarship to go to Moscow (seeing an advertisement in the *Times of India*). He was selected in 1967. He chose mining as his specialty (exploitation of hard mineral deposits, metal mining).

After returning from Moscow, there has been no looking back for Ganga Raju. Improving the quality of education in his hometown is his passion now. This is what drives him and makes his life meaningful.

Ravi Gupta

Ravi Gupta comes from humble beginnings. He grew up in New Delhi, India, with three brothers and two sisters. He did not come from a wealthy family but was taught the value of education and hard work by his father from a young age.

Ravi emigrated to Australia in 1981. He has been living in Sydney for the past 40 years. He has run (and continues to run) numerous successful businesses and holds a large property portfolio. He is today among some of the richest Indians in Sydney.

Ravi considers himself an educated risk-taker when it comes to business and investment and has demonstrated a high level of entrepreneurship over the years. A combination of technical skills, business acumen and a never-say-die attitude towards life and business has allowed him to establish himself on sound financial footing.

Ravi is a voracious reader and is well-versed in current domestic and international politics and business affairs. Ravi's greatest joys in life are his family and cricket. He is an avid philanthropist and has donated a significant proportion of this wealth to various charities over the years, especially to charities working with young children in rural India.

Raghu Puri

Raghu Puri is from Patel Hall (chemical engineering batch of 1982-86). He is a former VP of Cisco Systems USA and is currently a CEO of a multinational firm. He successfully started and sold a start-up in the USA. This gave him financial security for the rest of his life and the freedom to do what he liked to do. While his parents gave him values in his early years, his four years at IIT Kharagpur gave him the foundation for the rest of his life. At IIT, he developed the confidence to do anything, learnt business management and fiscal responsibility through campus projects, and acquired leadership skills through student representation at IIT Senate. The relationships forged in Patel Hall stood as support during a traumatic personal event and became the catalyst of a fortuitous opportunity that propelled him to the US. These bonds have prevailed over the past 30 years of his career spanning global leadership roles across Sprint, Cisco and Accenture. Strengthened through social media, these relationships provided an opportunity to organise support globally to give back to IIT and Patel Hall.

Dr. Srikanta Bandyopadhyay

Dr. Srikanta Bandyopadhyay was an M. Tech student at IIT Kanpur during 1971-1973. Srikanta did a two-year M. Tech course in materials science, after taking an official leave from his position at ISRO/SSTC Trivandrum, Department of Materials and Quality Control. The M. Tech course at IIT Kanpur helped him proceed in his career and specialise in composites, nanomaterials and recycling technology.

Srikanta is an avid singer and a music composer, for which he has received many appreciation letters, including one from IIT Kharagpur.

Rameshwar K. Maini

Rameshwar's story is the story of a youth from Ludhiana, Punjab who left home as a 16-year-old boy, entered IIT Bombay, and came out a man. From facing trials and tribulations due to his desire to become a successful singer, in a day and age when finding piles of money on the street was more likely than making it big in the music industry, to becoming a successful businessman, who is the CEO of his own engineering firm, Rameshwar's life is the stuff of dreams.

IIT Bombay not only gave him the education, confidence and social connections required to create a strong foundation for a successful future, but it also provided every brick needed to build his company Zentech Inc. Recently, Zentech, in partnership with Blue Whale Ocean Filtration, developed vessels that are specifically designed for the removal of microplastics from lakes, rivers and oceans.

Sundaram 'Sundy' Srinivasan

Sundaram 'Sundy' Srinivasan obtained a mechanical engineering degree from IIT School at MIT in Boston. He holds the position of Chief Operating Officer for Zentech Inc in Houston, Texas.

Sundaram has been actively involved in the activities of IIT alumni for close to 20 years. He was the founding president of the IIT Alumni of Greater Houston. He has also been the President of PanIIT USA.

He has lived and worked in many countries during a long career with Schlumberger, prior to joining Zentech.

His poetry has been published in a few anthologies. He also does standup comedy as a hobby; he has performed at many PanIIT conferences.

Sundaram is active in the local community and is involved in community theatre. He also loves interacting with the younger generation and coaching students and guiding them through the complex college application process.

IIT Kharagpur to Columbia University

Davender Jain

1964-1969, B. Tech - Mechanical Engineering, Nehru Hall, IIT Kharagpur

> *This is a story of hard work and intelligence and how they paid Davender, particularly when his father's rich business empire came to an end, following the rise of ULFA and SULFA terrorists in Assam.*
>
> *The story of Davender Jain is a story of taking risks in life and handling situations and jobs as diverse as they can be, by moving from Assam to the USA then back to India, then to the World Bank and then to the UN. After being posted as an advisor to work for the Parliament of NSW in Sydney, he decided to settle down in Australia.*

I was in the last batch of Senior Cambridge, whose high-school classes were held in top-notch Indian schools, but the final examination papers went to Cambridge University in England for evaluation. Senior Cambridge exams were held in December each year, whereas IIT's entrance exams followed the Indian high-school system and were held much later. This gave the Senior Cambridge students an opportunity to fill the gap in their learning for the IIT entrance exams, as the coverage of mathematics and other subjects was much less in Senior Cambridge compared to the higher secondary exams of India. In my case, it so happened that I realised much later that I need to do extra preparation for the IIT exams. A day before the first exam, the stress built up so much that I was running temperature. Nevertheless, I couldn't afford to not take the exams. On the second day of the exams, in the last paper, I answered almost all the questions. Then I came to the last question, for which I knew the answer, but due to the fever, I just couldn't write anymore and skipped it. Then the results came. My rank was 62 in the whole of India! Being in the top 100 in India has its own privileges. In the interview, almost every representative from every IIT was telling me the plus points at their institute and why I should join them. I could take any branch of engineering in any IIT of my choice. The Delhi IIT representative said that their food was very good and that the campus was in my hometown. The representatives from Kanpur, Bombay and Madras too listed out the advantages of joining their institute. Only Kharagpur's representative kept quiet.

In those days, mechanical engineering was the most sought-after branch. I chose mechanical engineering in IIT Kharagpur because it was the most reputed institute in those days and all my school friends were going there. In our days, the IITs were not known to the Ivy League colleges in the USA. Even the topmost student from IIT Kharagpur barely had a chance to get into an Ivy League college. This fact was known to all of us. I was one of the lucky ones to make it based on my almost perfect scores in GRE and SAT.

At Columbia

I landed in New York with $29 in my pocket on a nice summer's day in August 1969. I was received by a Columbia University representative at the airport and put up in a hotel near the university. After paying $25 for the night stay, I had just $4 left in my pocket. However, I had no worries and focused on the bright future ahead of me. The next day, I met a fellow Indian student in campus who was looking for a roommate. It was decided that I would share his accommodation and he agreed for me to pay him when I had money.

Before going to the USA, my brother-in-law, who was a Harvard Law graduate, advised me to study hard as getting a degree from an Ivy League college was a once-in-a-lifetime opportunity. Study hard I did, for a change. The result was that, upon graduation, I was awarded the Citation for Outstanding Achievement as a graduate student. This was followed by a membership to Alpha Pi Mu honour society, the fellowship of Columbia University, and so on.

Back to India

Having graduated from Columbia with a Distinguished Alumni Award and the Fellow of Columbia University decorating my collar, I was called by one of the senior directors of Tata Group, who was based in New York. He offered me a job in India. But I had no intention of going back to India in the near future. He said, nevertheless, I could pay him a visit to Bombay and meet the director, Mr Kohli, on my next visit to Delhi. I said the Tatas would only provide me airfare from Delhi to Bombay and back to Delhi and that I could go only if they arranged a hotel for me too. He agreed. During the next visit to Delhi, I phoned Mr Kohli and he said Mr Tobaccowala had spoken to him and, yes, they would provide me a return airfare and pay for my stay in Bombay. I thought there was no harm in going and seeing Bombay and so I went.

TCS was based in one big hall in the Air India building at Nariman Point, Bombay. I was made to sit in the library and appear for an exam. I refused to take the exam and said that I already had a job in New York and wanted to go back there. The human resources manager virtually begged me to take the exam and so I succumbed. There were a few other US-returned postgraduates taking the exam. After the exam, I was taken for lunch and then to Bombay House (the headquarters of the Tata empire) to meet the chairman of Tata Sons, Mr Aggarwal. After finishing the meeting, I was driven back to Mr Kohli's office. It was 6 pm by then and I was called straight in. I saw a rather overpowering personality with a big moustache sitting behind a big desk. He opened the discussion by saying, "Mr Jain, you have been approved by three directors (including himself) and you have done very well in the exam. We want to make you an offer." With the kind of personality that Mr Kohli had, I just couldn't say. "Sorry sir, I had come to Bombay for just a holiday!" Instead,

I told him that finding housing in Bombay was very difficult. He straightaway replied that they would lease a one-bedroom flat for me in Pali Hills, Nariman Point. He also offered a salary almost twice that of what they normally offered to a person with a similar background. He also said I would work with the acquisitions and mergers team of Tata Sons. I told him that I would think about the offer and let him know the next day.

In the evening, I phoned my father to break the news to him. He said, "Just take it." I told him that I wanted to go back to the US. He was upset and said he would go on a 'hunger strike' if I didn't accept the job. I had no choice. So, for the next two years, it was Bombay for me.

I enjoyed the job as it involved going 'suited-booted' to various cities, staying in five-star hotels and assessing the possibilities of new ventures and acquisition of sick companies. However, Bombay didn't suit me. Slow traffic resulting in hours of driving to work and other issues did not help.

While in the acquisitions and mergers team, I worked on a feasibility report for the Industrial Development Bank of India (IDBI), an affiliate of the Reserve Bank of India, for a medium-sized public limited company. The company was to re-melt iron scrap and convert it into iron rods used in construction. The project was supposedly for young entrepreneur engineers in the industrially backward states of India. Considering the fact that my father had two factories and other businesses in Assam, I thought this would be a perfect project for me to start in Assam. There was no such facility in Assam and all the scrap iron used to go to Calcutta and iron rods were brought from there.

I went to Assam, floated a public limited company, applied for funding from IDBI, and was in the process of negotiations with them when my father had a severe heart attack. My elder brother was looking after the business in Assam and my younger brother was studying in IIT-D. So, I was with my father for almost two years in Delhi until he was hale and hearty and ready to go back to Assam. On recovery, my father told me that he was not in a state of mind to start a new venture, particularly in the face of rising threat from ULFA. My elder brother was not supportive too. So, the dream of starting the project went up in smoke.

I had lost two precious years and didn't want to go back to Assam and join the existing business. One of the factors was also that the ULFA/SULFA extortionists were becoming stronger day by day. The local Assamese people supported them because they thought the Government of India was not doing enough for them. Assam produced all the oil and tea in India, yet it was not being looked after. However, the way I saw it was the extortionists' aim was not to help Assam or the Assamese people but to pocket the money coming from Pakistan through East Pakistan (now Bangladesh) and extort more from Marwaris, who owned not only the tea gardens but virtually every other business. A Kashmir-style of exodus started in Assam by the Marwaris and other businessmen, as well as Bengalis, who occupied all the important jobs. Both my brothers had to flee overnight to Delhi, where fortunately my father had built a big house, nearly in the heart of the city, with 16 rooms and 4 large halls. Our factories in Assam were burnt and trucks that carried stones from our stone crushing plant were also burnt. Remaining to date is our bungalow, one *gawala ghar*—a big piece of land for growing vegetables and housing cows and where some of our employees lived, and a petrol pump. **This is a little-known story of exodus of Indians from their very own India, which is hardly talked about.**

A new life-changing venture

My last job in India was with Punjab Markfed in Chandigarh. Punjab Markfed had 1000 branches in Punjab through which it procured wheat, rice and cotton, to name a few crops, and distributed fertilisers, seeds and other agricultural inputs to farmers. In addition, it had 22 agro processing plants, for making products such as granulated NPK, pesticides and water pipes. However, there was no information system in place to monitor the plants as well as the field activities such as procurement of wheat on a particular day or distribution of fertilisers. I put in place a computer-based digital management information system, supported by wireless network. This was the first case of digitisation in India.

A tale of immense challenges with significant outcomes

This is a story of challenges and hurdles, overcoming old attitudes and changing the profit-and-loss account of a major Indian corporation through one of the first attempts of computerisation in India.

The company was Punjab Markfed and the time was the early 80s. I had the fortune of being a major change agent. Punjab Markfed, a co-operative and one of the largest corporations in India with 6000 employees in the late 70s-early 80s, had a turnover of Rs 1000 crore. It had 22 agro processing plants and 1000 branch offices for agricultural produce procurement and agro input distribution, with 40 main centres and 12 district offices. The head office was in Chandigarh. The processing plants were engaged in cement pipe manufacturing, pesticide formulation, NPK production, cotton seed processing and vanaspati ghee making, among others. Corruption was rampant as there was no information to control the operations in branch offices or in any of the agro processing plants.

As an example, when wheat arrived in *mandis*, railway wagons had to be arranged to take the wheat to the warehouses in other parts of India; funds also had to be arranged to pay the farmers. For this, timely information was needed at the district offices and the head office. Similarly, at the time of planting, adequate supply of fertiliser of the type required had to be arranged. Due to lack of information, there were times when a store manager would sell the wheat privately, set fire to the warehouse and records, and run away. He would later take the plea that someone set fire to the warehouse and all records were burnt in the fire. There was virtually no evidence to prosecute him.

I was hired to set up an information system at the head office so that the 12 district offices would know and control what was going on in the field. This was a rather tall order and the task was not easy. It meant not only receiving accurate information but also receiving it in a timely manner. For example, information on wheat arrivals in all the *mandis* in the state and funds availability to pay the farmers had to be received daily from 1000 centres for the previous day at the head office. Some of this information was politically sensitive and was required by the chief minister on a daily basis. There was no Wi-Fi in the early 80s and Hindustan Computers Limited (HCL) had just started manufacturing desktop computers in India. It was suggested that wireless sets could perhaps be used for the timely flow of information from 40 major centres to the 12 district offices and from the district offices to the head office in Chandigarh. However, as Punjab was a state bordering Pakistan, getting a wireless licence was next to impossible.

My first step was to design an information system in terms of the information to be generated at the branch level, the major centre level, the district level and then head office level. Simultaneously, how the information would flow and how it would be stored, collated, analysed and used had to be designed. Hardware requirements for these tasks had to be worked out. Lastly, the staff had to be trained to do the job without errors and in a timely manner. Implementation at 1000 branches, 40 major centres, 12 district offices and finally at the head office was a Herculean task by any measure. The good thing was that I had the complete unconditional support of the CEO, all the way. A blank cheque.

I started off by getting a couple of consultants from PWC to design the system. A thorough understanding of how the procurement, storage and distribution of agricultural commodities took place at the grass roots level had to be ensured to make the designed system practical. This was also true for the distribution of agro products such as fertilisers, pesticides and seeds. There were 'catches' in the system that had to be understood. For example, when the wheat was procured, it had a certain weight. As we get closer to the rainy season, which followed harvesting, wheat absorbed moisture and gained weight. For example, the weight of 100 kg of wheat procured could be around 110 kg or so at the time of sales. On procurement of 10,000 tonnes of wheat, there could be 1000 kg that the branch could sell 'privately'. Such things had to be built into the system to prevent malpractices.

In parallel with the system design, obtaining licence for procurement of wireless equipment was initiated. Obtaining the licence from the Government of India was a major hurdle. Fortunately, the speaker of the Indian Parliament was from Punjab and, after a lot of lobbying and innumerable visits to Delhi, we finally got a licence. Punjab Wireless was a state government undertaking in Punjab, and the order was placed with them for one set each for all the major 40 centres, 12 district offices and the head office. HCL had just come out with their 'System 4', which was a powerful indigenous desktop computer at that time. An order was placed for 40 HCL systems for major centres, 12 for each of the 12 district offices and one for the head office. Setting up of wireless/computer rooms and staff training commenced. At the same time, an effective administrative system was devised, whereby if a centre did not send the information accurately or in a timely manner, strict action could be taken against the staff responsible.

The system-designed information, in a prescribed format, would be sent by each of the 1000 branch offices, by a courier, to one of the 40 centres under which it came. The courier was usually a staff member who went by bus. He would collect the report from the centres falling on the way.

Another staff would be standing at the bus stop ready with the report and he would quickly drop it in the designated bag of the courier sitting in the bus. This way, all the 1000 centres were to send reports to 40 major centres and ensure they reached the designated major centre on the same day. The 40 major centres were to enter the reports on the desktop computer and wire the consolidated report to 12 district offices. The 12 district offices did the same thing and the report reached the head office early next day. For instance, all the information on close of business on 15th March was sent by the branches on 16th March early morning. It would be entered into a computer during the day and transmitted by wireless to reach the head office on 17th March early morning. It would be on the desk of each functional manager before he arrived in the Chandigarh office at 9 am on 17th March. Those commodities that were in 'season' were reported daily, others on a weekly basis, and some even on a monthly basis.

Not everything went as planned. Markfed's labour union was watching the new system closely. In those days, in the 80s, it was commonly believed in India that introducing computers could result in job losses. As a 34 years young (and confident) professional, I faced the wrath of the union and was asked to explain the new system to the board and how it would not cut jobs but bring in transparency, improve efficiency and result in greater profits.

The system was approved by the board, though the labour union was still against it. There was a director who saw an opportunity for himself. He did not belong to the ruling party. He took his car and went to Delhi. Delhi was on alert due to the Khalistan movement simmering in Punjab those days. This director expressed his willingness to change horses and support the party ruling in Delhi, provided he was made the CEO of Punjab Markfed.

The CEO of Punjab Markfed was a politically sensitive post as it not only provided direct employment to 6000 people but also affected the life of almost all farmers in one way or the other. His proposal was accepted. He came back to Chandigarh, had a notice posted outside the CEO's office declaring that the current CEO should report to the Punjab secretariat, and he was to take charge in his place.

The next morning, the first thing he did was to call me and blame me for all the things that had gone wrong in the company. He also said that he wanted the new system to be scrapped. He not only wanted to appease the union, but he was also not interested in transparency and was quite happy with the middlemen (including himself) making a buck. I told him that the system could not be scrapped as the advance had been paid for the hardware and, under the contract, the suppliers had the right not to return the advance paid.

Based on this work, I was called to Bombay by a team of World Bank officials who had heard about my pioneering efforts and was made an offer that I could not turn down. In summary, it included a big house in a top locality with no rent to pay, a car with a driver with no fuel expenses, driver's salary and petrol costs, no electricity or telephone bills to pay, no school fees for my two children at a prestigious international school, no house/land taxes of any sort, and, on top of it all, a living allowance in local currency, which was equal to three times the salary of a top bureaucrat like a secretary in the government. To top it all, there would be a salary in US dollars, paid overseas in any bank/country of my choice. All tax-free! Sitting in my study room at home (furnished with mahogany furniture), I used to think many times, *"Bhagwan jab deta hein to chappar phad kar deta hein."* This is an Indian saying that means 'when God gives, it rains money from the roof'.

Australia

After completing several overseas assignments with the World Bank and finally being the UN advisor in Ghana, I served the Parliament of NSW, Sydney, Australia from 1992 onwards. A parliamentary committee was set up to repeal all the regulations in blocks (say everything made before 1962 in one go, another block made between 1962 to 1972 to go next year and so on); the concerned government departments were to remake them after assessing their costs and the benefits for the society. There were two professional officers deputed with the committee to examine each new regulation and submit its report to the committee. The committee had the power, delegated from the parliament, to 'make' the regulations and then just table them in the house. I was to advise on social costs and benefits of the new regulation on society, and my colleague's role was to ascertain the legality of the new regulation. This was a challenging job for me, but, with the confidence that IIT Kharagpur had instilled in me, learning was fast and soon I made my mark, with several of my reports tabled in the parliament, approved and archived. I liked Australia and decided to stay back here.

Finally, my work with the Parliament of NSW took me to social and economic evaluation of public sector investment projects (mostly infrastructure), risk management as well as midterm/post-completion reviews. This suited well with my engineering background. I set up my own company in 2005 to do these tasks as a consultant and immediately I had loads of work from the public and private sector, which wanted these services. For the public sector, it was a statutory requirement for all projects over $10 million. So, there was no dearth of work. Added to this were assignments from my former employer, the World Bank, which kept coming. A couple need mention here—restructure of the IT sector in Fiji following privatisation and a risk management plan for Khan Bank in Mongolia. Restructure of the IT sector in Fiji meant working for almost a year with the chairman of Fiji's regulatory authority, as a counterpart, and reporting to the World Bank. The Mongolia assignment involved putting in a risk management system for the largest bank of Mongolia, which was to be provided funding by the Asian Development Bank.

I thought Australia was a country with temperate weather (no snowfall). This was a 'lucky' country, as the English called it, and a country where everyone was a migrant.

It was also a country that had struck a good balance between socialism and capitalism, with almost no crime. I decided to settle down in Australia.

A film on IIT Kharagpur

My story will not be complete without mentioning a project that was close to my heart. I had seen several short videos of a producer (herein referred to as KAG to hide the actual identity) and thought a film on IIT Kharagpur made by KAG would be a good idea. I emailed my proposal to the producer. Apparently, they did some research on IITs and then promptly replied to me in the affirmative. I thought the IIT Kharagpur Foundation USA (referred to as 'Foundation') would be the best body to take up this project. As I knew the key people running the Foundation from my IIT days, they quickly agreed to it. However, for reasons that I was not told, the Foundation pulled out before KAG were all set to go to the USA. This left me with great frustration. I not only had to the pay the airfare for three people but also faced a host of other issues. A significant issue was this: from which account would the payment be made and how to make progress payment? KAG pleaded with me not to pull out of the project and promised to cooperate fully.

On trust, I decided to progress with the project alone and let the money go into KAG account directly. There was no time to get a contractor to set up a bank account to progressively disburse money to KAG, based on the progress of the film. The Foundation had a charitable bank account that was not available to me. During the Foundation days, every person to be interviewed for the film was to deposit $1000 in the Foundation's account. I scrapped this policy, as I thought that the selection of the person to be interviewed had to be on merit, rather than based on the money paid. Also, I let the voluntary contribution go into KAG's account directly. The project progressed smoothly; some alumni made contributions to the project, and I continued to make sure KAG was adequately compensated for the time as well as the out-of-pocket expenses. One alumnus provided boarding/lodging and airfare to KAG to visit his city. Notably, after KAG left the city, the alumnus called me and said, "Davender, be careful of these fellows, lest you are cheated!"

The director of IIT Kharagpur (PPC those days) agreed to support the project. However, he said the film should not glorify anyone. I took this seriously and told KAG not to highlight me or even mention me. This was also in Jainism's system—not to disclose the name of the donor.

A tour of more than two months all over the USA (including a visit to Hawaii) was a rather costly affair. But KAG were also filming other videos from other assignments in the USA, which they never mentioned to me. Anyhow, I paid much more than the promised and agreed amount to KAG for the film.

Finally the film saw the light of the day in February 2019.

The film was a huge success. It has had 8 lakh (0.8 million) views on YouTube till date.

Life In Different Campuses: Pan-India and across the Globe

Ganesh Prasad

1983-1985, B. Tech - Civil Engineering, IIT Madras

> *Ganesh Prasad spent his childhood in the quiet and green IISc Bangalore campus, where his father was a professor. Ganesh shares his experiences and learnings in the hope that they will be useful and encouraging to younger people on the threshold of their tertiary education or working life. Some of his insights into the positives and negatives of India's elite institutions of learning may also be interesting to readers.*

I guess mine is a somewhat unique story because I have lived on the campuses of four of India's prestigious institutes—IIT-M, IIM-A, IIT-K and IISc.

Early childhood and teens

My father was a professor at the Indian Institute of Science, Bangalore; so my childhood was spent on that campus.

Right after my B. Tech, I did my MBA (PGDM) at IIM Ahmedabad from 1985 to 1987.

After five years of working in the IT industry, I went back to school at IIT Kanpur to do my M. Tech in computer science, from June 1992 to December 1993.

Let me share some of my impressions about these institutes as I describe my life's journey.

When one enters the quiet and green campus of IISc Bangalore, from the bustling main road outside, there is a sudden hush and the temperature drops perceptibly. It's a compact campus with departments, faculty quarters and student hostels, all within comfortable walking distance of one another. My younger sister and I grew up in this idyllic environment. As children of professors, my friends and I wandered all over the campus, enjoying its many facilities, including the massive library, gymkhana and swimming pool.

I guess growing up as the son of a scientist, within the campus of an institution devoted to science, surrounded by friends whose parents were also professors of science, unconsciously influenced my career preferences. There was no doubt in my mind that I would do my degree in a scientific discipline.

In 1980, I wrote the JEE and managed to get admission in the hallowed IIT, with a middling sort of rank (655).

This may seem like a logical progression of events and a relatively smooth sailing, but it almost didn't happen.

Looking back, I can see that there have been two major turning points in my life that have brought me to where I am. I will talk about the second one later on, but the first turning point happened during my school days and threatened to upend the comfortable life I had known until that point.

My father fell seriously ill in 1975, when I was 12 years old. He did recover eventually and went on to live for another 33 years. But when I think about how things could have turned out, I realise how different my life would have been after that and what a different person I would have become.

My father survived his serious illness and continued on at IISc until his retirement. This was the first critical juncture of my life. I guess it was a non-turning point, important for what almost happened but did not.

I don't think I would have made it into IIT if my dad hadn't been around. He helped me immensely with my preparation for the JEE.

If I ever got stuck on a maths or physics problem, he would ask me not to waste time on it but mark it on the question booklet and move on to the next problem. He would sit up and solve the leftover problems overnight and show me the solutions the next morning.

So, I owe my admission into IIT not just to the iconic Agrawal classes but also to the support of my dad, who could easily have passed the JEE himself. Not many students have had such a good fortune.

After the initial jubilation over my JEE result, it came down to the decision of which of the five IITs to choose. All of them were considered equally good; so proximity became the sole criterion. The closest IIT to Bangalore was at Madras (now Chennai), an overnight train journey away. Thinking back on that period from my current home on another continent altogether, it seems strange that my parents would feel so concerned about their 17-year-old son living 'so far away', when they were just two adjacent cities in South India. I guess that was middle-class India back then.

The IIT Madras years

This was 1980, and although most other engineering colleges in the country had already switched over to the four-year degree format, the IITs had not yet done so. Ours was to be the last of the five-year batches.

In our batch of 250 students, only 3 were girls. Engineering was unfortunately seen as a male profession back then, and not many girls would even sit for the entrance exam.

IIT-M was probably unique among all the IITs in providing single rooms to all students right from the first year; so I never had to share a room with anyone. The rooms were bare, with just a wooden desk and a metal bed. The students had to bring their own bedclothes, their own table fans to deal with the infamous Madras summers, and a plastic bucket. As I was to discover later, those buckets became lifesavers because of the frequent water shortages in Madras.

Every student kept a bucket full of water in their room to deal with 'emergencies'.

The IIT-M campus was unique in one respect. There were chital deer and blackbuck roaming around, and it was a common sight to see these animals calmly crossing the road in front of us as we cycled to and from class.

Unlike a few others who felt homesick in the early days, I took to hostel life like a duck to water. Not having parents around to constantly tell me to study was a great relief, and I'm sorry to say that I enjoyed my freedom so much that I hardly ever studied, except just before the exams. My grades reflected the study habits, and I mostly had Cs on my grade card.

I had no particular reason for choosing civil engineering from among all the branches I was eligible for. I thought it sounded more interesting, and my parents didn't object to my choice. Later on, I met another student who said he had selected chemical engineering because it was easier to get admission and financial aid to study at a US university with a degree in chemical engineering. Such long-term planning to go to the US even before joining the undergraduate programme! I had never thought so far ahead. By the end of my B. Tech, I realised just how single-minded and competitive an IIT-M student could be when it came to career progress.

Soon I found that even the IIT-M academic system encouraged this hyper-competitive attitude. Grades were not based on one's absolute marks but they were relative to the class median. Relative grading led to unhealthy peer competition. The class toppers were often blamed, only half-jokingly, for raising the class median and thereby condemning others to lower grades. Studying hard was, therefore, referred to as an 'anti-social' activity, but everyone did it surreptitiously. (Except people like me of course, who helped in lowering the class median.)

There was also an unhealthy culture of snobbery based on branches and grades, a kind of casteism if you will. Those studying electronics were the elites. Those in civil engineering and naval architecture were the bottom-feeders. Another jolt came after the grades of the first semester were out. The 9-pointers were demi-gods, admired and hated at the same time. The 6-pointers were treated with contempt. This was one of the negative aspects of IIT-M's student culture.

As I said earlier, ours was the last of the five-year batches. My batchmates realised that with the next B. Tech batch having a four-year programme, two batches would end up graduating in the same year—1985. There would be twice the competition for everything, whether it was for jobs, US university admissions or IIM admissions. After a lot of lobbying from representatives of our batch, the institute's administration agreed to make ours an 'accelerated programme'. We would be allowed to take one extra course every semester from the fourth semester onwards, so that we could complete all the credits required for the degree by the end of the ninth semester. So, our batch managed to squeeze through the gap between the 1979-84 batch and the 1981-85 batch. We were known as the 4.5-year B. Techs.

A word about academics at IIT-M, and this is probably true of the other IITs as well. There were hardly any exams with essay-type questions. Every test and exam involved solving quantitative problems. If you could demonstrate your understanding of theory by solving an actual problem, then you got marks, not otherwise. Later on, I learnt, to my surprise, that students from other engineering colleges had to answer essay-type questions like the one made famous by the Bollywood movie *3 Idiots*—How does an induction motor start?

No IIT exam would ever have such a question. It would be more like this: *An induction motor has 'n' coils of such-and-such a radius and an applied current of 'x' amps. Calculate the maximum torque developed by the motor.* This is probably why IITs were considered unique in India.

In fact, it was a lightbulb moment for me when we had our first physics tutorial. It's a habit of Indian students to ask this very basic question: "Sir, what should we assume as the value of 'g' (acceleration due to gravity)?" In junior college, lecturers would oblige by saying "9.81 metres/second-squared" or something like that. My IIT professor just said, "Any reasonable value," and that was that. I suddenly understood what was really being expected of us. It wasn't the exact value of the answer that was important. It was the knowledge of how to solve a problem.

There is a drawback of Indian engineering education that I will point out here, and this is true of the IITs as well. Education is still theoretical. Yes, IIT students may be better at quantitative problem-solving as opposed to regurgitating definitions and descriptions, but most of them cannot change a an actual lightbulb. We don't get to work with our hands in spite of all the labs and workshops we attend. After migrating to Australia and talking to people here, I realised that engineering education in other countries was much more practical. Engineering graduates in other countries can actually build things with their hands and not just solve equations. I hope things have changed for the better in India since I graduated.

As we got to the sixth and seventh semesters, preparations for post-graduation life were in full swing. Unlike at other IITs, the Indian Administrative Service (IAS) was not one of the favoured career options at IIT-M. It was either higher studies in the US or an MBA at one of the IIMs. Very few chose to take up a job in the industry. It was said that there was a runway at IIT Madras whose flight path led straight to the US and a highway that led to the IIMs. The way IIT-M students used to prepare for these competitive exams and group discussions was scary to watch. Every night after dinner, an entire batch would occupy the empty mess hall and sit quietly in rows while one student would display flashcards and get others to answer vocabulary questions. This was in preparation for GRE.

Applying to US universities was also done in a highly coordinated manner. The class topper would be asked the names of his top-two preferred universities. Then he alone would apply to these two universities. The second-ranker would then be asked for his two preferences, and so on. Each engineering department of a US university would then receive exactly one application from the whole of IIT Madras. Needless internal competition was avoided, and almost everyone of the students managed to secure admission and financial aid. IIT-M had turned US university applications into a fine art!

Group discussions for admission to the IIMs were no different. Woe unto the non-IIT-M candidate in the city of Madras who found themselves in the same room as a bunch of IIT-M students. The IIT-M guys would monopolise the conversation and only pass the 'baton' to one another, not allowing the others to even speak. It was cut-throat!

By the time I reached the final year of my B. Tech, I realised that my heart was not into civil engineering, and I couldn't see myself either working in the field or doing an MS or a PhD in civil enginerring, as most of my batchmates had decided to do. Fortunately, there was a face-saving way out—the IIMs. IIT-IIM types did have to endure mild taunts about being 'engineers who sold soap', but it was socially respectable.

My studious preparation for the CAT entrance exam paid off, and I received interview calls to all three of the then IIMs (A, B and C).

I was back home in Bangalore at the time of the IIM interviews; so I didn't get the benefit of the IIT-M shark pack during the group discussions, but I still managed to secure admission to all three IIMs. One of my IIT-M batchmates, who was also from Bangalore, chose

IIM Bangalore because it was home, but something in me didn't let me settle for that easy option. IIM Ahmedabad had been consistently ranked as the best B-school in India; so I succumbed to the lure of that label.

The IIM Ahmedabad years

IIM-A was a much, much more compact campus than the sprawling one we knew at IIT-M. At IIT-M, we couldn't survive without a bicycle. At IIM-A, it was impossible to use a bicycle because of the number of staircases everywhere. And there was no need for bikes anyway. Our classes and the library were very close to the dorms where we stayed. My dorm was literally a hundred metres from my classroom.

The architecture of the buildings at IIM-A was distinct, with an exposed brick facade. Some of us joked that the institute must have run out of funds before a decent coat of plaster could be applied. It's good that the architect Louis Kahn couldn't hear what we philistines were saying about his work.

About half of all the students at IIM-A were engineers, about a third being IITians. (A guy from IIT Delhi called Raghuram Rajan was my batchmate.) The rest were Cas and B.Com and BA (economics) degree holders. The proportion of girls at IIM-A was higher than at IIT-M. There were 18 girls in our batch of 174 students, a better ratio than 3 out of 250, but still nowhere near parity.

There was also a subtle shift of academic gears when we moved from IIT to IIM.

IITs were heavily quantitative, of course. IIM-A was also quantitative in many subjects, but every subject was taught using the case-study method. If exam questions at IIT followed the pattern of asking questions like 'calculate the torque' (or bending moment or shear force), cases at IIM-A would generally end with this question: 'What should the company do?'

One of my IIT-M friends who joined IIM-A with me had a sudden epiphany, "*Machan*, this place is just like IIT! Instead of kilograms, joules or volts, it's rupees!" I had a good laugh at that, but there was a lot of truth in his observation. IIT was fundamentally about physical stuff, while IIM was fundamentally about money. But everything was approached in the same way –with logic, reason and calculation.

I should mention that I had an important and humbling learning experience at IIM-A. I confess I went there with a certain amount of arrogance as an IITian and more basically as an engineer. I had this impression that only engineers knew how to think. But as the case studies rolled on and I heard my classmates from non-engineering backgrounds arguing points logically and coherently, my respect for them increased, and I realised that engineers did not have a monopoly on intellect. There are many kinds of intelligence, and many important problems in life do not require the ability to solve mathematical equations.

My personal dismay at IIM-A was the realisation that I still hadn't found my calling. A medical career had never been an option for me because I couldn't handle the thought of surgery and blood; so I had run away from medicine into the arms of engineering, the only other career option available at the time. It had taken me a few years to realise that I didn't want engineering as a career either; so I ran away from engineering into the arms of business management. And now, I was beginning to have that awful feeling all over again. Finance and accounting was a nightmare. To this day, I cannot seem to get a balance sheet to balance.

Marketing was a different beast altogether. I had this almost moral revulsion for the profession, which I haven't completely shed to this day. Marketing always struck me as being a somewhat evil function, in that it seemed designed to make people want things they didn't need. I began to refer to it in the North Indian reduplicative style i.e. "marketing-sharketing".

But all that left me with no career options. Even after studying at two of the most prestigious educational institutes in the country, I still did not know what I was going to do with my life. I was in despair.

And then, with a heavenly blare of trumpets, the third trimester of the first year began, and one of the subjects was CDPS (Computers and Data Processing Systems).

We had been taught the FORTRAN programming language at IIT-M, and I had scored a C grade as usual. But somewhere along the way, I learnt BASIC programming. My father had taught himself BASIC, and he passed on his knowledge to me. He was particularly excited about a feature of the language that I would later learn was taboo—the GOTO statement. So I had learnt how to write code at the time I was reintroduced to computer programming at IIM-A.

CDPS was just the medicine I needed. We were taught BASIC, but it was introduced in a much more disciplined way, using a structured syntax called pseudocode. When I combined my raw knowledge of programming with the discipline of pseudocode, I found myself turning out much more elegant programs that worked on the first go. I remember a class test where we were asked to transpose a matrix. I realised that I could repeat the read loop as the write loop and simply change $A(i,j)$ to $A(j,i)$. I handed in my paper and was out of the room in five minutes, to the shock of the rest of the class, and I got full marks to boot.

Suddenly, I had celebrity status. Other students started coming to me for help with their programming assignments, something I had never experienced in years. More importantly, I had found my calling at last.

In fact, the four things that are together called Ikigai came together for me. Computer programming was something I enjoyed, something I was good at, something the world needed, and something the world was willing to pay for. The timing was just right. Prime Minister Rajiv Gandhi's liberalisation and computerisation drives had just begun, and the IT sector in India began to see explosive growth starting from the mid-80s.

And that's how in 1987, during the campus placement interviews at the end of my two years at IIM-A, I got a job as a programmer at my dream company, CMC Ltd.

The CMC Bombay years

I had never lived in Bombay before, and there was something in the air in that city that was infectious—the crackling energy, the egalitarianism, the pervasive can-do attitude, and the unique Bombay sense of humour.

CMC had the best corporate culture I have ever experienced. It wasn't a stodgy bureaucracy as one would expect of a government company, and it didn't have the mercenary, exploitative edge of a private company. The friendships I made at CMC have lasted to this day.

I stayed on in CMC without a thought about the future, simply because I loved the place (both Bombay and CMC Bombay). Most of my colleagues only stayed a couple of years before leaving for the US. CMC delivered so many large turnkey projects using cutting-edge technology that even a two-year stint there was enough to give a young software professional an enviable CV. One of my colleagues joked about the CMC experience, "*Do saal ka course hai.*" (It's a two-year course.) That's because everyone seemed to graduate and leave after a couple of years, once they got the right technologies onto their CV.

Except me. I was just happy being there.

But then something happened after four years in CMC that was to profoundly change my life. This was the second turning point of my life that I had referred to at the beginning.

In mid-1991, I was sent to Mauritius on a short consulting assignment. One of my managers made a passing suggestion that I should request admin to book my return ticket via Singapore, so that I could take a short break and do some sightseeing. As it happened, the three-way ticket via Singapore was about 500 rupees more expensive than the two-way return ticket from Bombay to Mauritius, but it was typical of CMC's generous corporate culture to pay the difference without a murmur.

No good deed goes unpunished, and CMC paid for my Singapore trip in more ways than one. I, who had never once thought of leaving India in spite of the advice and personal examples of many friends, suddenly found my mind blown at the cleanliness, order and convenience of a 'First World' country. Three days in Singapore, and my mind was made up. I wanted to leave India and live abroad. As I told my friends at the time, "CMC made a mistake by sending me abroad."

After discussing with many friends, I finally decided that the best country to migrate to would be Australia, and I submitted my application for permanent migration. But when I received a response to my application a few weeks later, it was an unexpected disappointment.

My degrees from prestigious institutes did not cut much ice with the Australian immigration department. As an IT professional, I was expected to have an IT-related degree from a recognised university. My civil engineering degree from IIT-M did not cut it. Neither did my PGDM from IIM-A, even though I had done a few courses in information systems.

I was dejected for a few days, and then I made the decision to go back to school, earn a degree in computer science, and reapply to migrate to Australia. Dear old CMC was willing to sponsor me for an M. Tech course at one of the IITs; so I gratefully took up that option and joined IIT Kanpur in June 1992. I guess it would have been much more convenient for me to join IIT Bombay or return to my alma mater IIT Madras, but snob value influenced my decision. The computer science department at IIT-K was rated the best among all the IITs at that time; so even though Kanpur was a fair way off, I gritted my teeth and did it for the sake of the label.

The IIT Kanpur years

There were 13 students in my M. Tech computer science batch, all men. Three were B. Techs from IIT Kanpur, and a couple of them were doing their M. Tech as a way of passing their time while preparing for the IAS exam and interview. I realised again the difference between IIT-M and the other IITs in that the IAS seemed to be a big thing everywhere else.

Now here's a little-known dynamic that exists within the IITs, between the B. Tech and the M. Tech students. B. Techs tend to feel a certain superiority vis-a-vis M. Techs, viewing them as 'second-try IITians', because those who couldn't get into IIT at the B. Tech level do their undergrad degrees at other engineering colleges and then reapply to the IITs to do their M. Tech. During my B. Tech days at IIT-M, I confess I shared that smug feeling of superiority, but the shoe was on the other foot when I joined IIT-K as an M. Tech student.

Mind you, my M. Tech batchmates were every bit as smart as anyone I knew, but there it is. The disdain among B. Techs for M. Techs is part of the dark cultural underbelly of the IITs. I was now conscious of this perception whenever I spoke to B. Tech students at my department, and I often felt compelled to mention at some point in the conversation that I had also done my B. Tech at an IIT.

Looking back, I can see how much insecurity I had in spite of having studied at an elite institution. Or perhaps it was precisely because of this. It's an important lesson to everyone not to be dazzled by the aura of India's elite institutions and to recognise the serpents that lurk in this paradise.

I didn't regret my decision to do an M. Tech, of course. The academic standards of the computer science department were high, and the equipment was quite modern. I was, however, disappointed at the limited scope of the curriculum at the M. Tech level. At a rough estimate, we must have done at least 30 core courses in our area of specialisation at the B. Tech level. The M. Tech programme was only three semesters long, and half the credits were devoted to project work. There were just six courses at the master's level, compared to over 30 at the undergrad level. I guess it made sense, because the programme was designed for those who had already studied computer science at the undergrad level, but for someone like me who had graduated in another branch and was hoping to catch up on the subjects in this area, there weren't too many opportunities. I tried to make up for this by auditing a couple of subjects that I was interested in.

Overall, I enjoyed my stay at IIT Kanpur. There was just one scary thing about the campus though. Once winter was over and the days got warmer, we got to see snakes everywhere; so, we really had to watch our step whenever we walked around, especially on the grass or in unpaved areas.

The biggest difference I found during my third stint studying at an elite Indian institute was in myself. I had never been interested in studies before, either in civil engineering or in management, and my mediocre grades reflected my indifference. But during my M. Tech days, to my own surprise, I found myself studying out of interest in the subject. Once again, my grades reflected my effort. I graduated from IIT-K with a GPA of 9.22 out of 10.

The in-between years

Once I completed my M. Tech and returned to CMC, I came under pressure from my parents to marry and 'settle down'. I went through the standard process of a modern arranged marriage, wherein the guy and girl get to specify the kind of partner they want and the parents facilitate their meeting by putting out ads and handling the initial correspondence. I met my future wife Sashi along with both sets of parents on the 2nd of March 1994. Sashi was a CA who could draw up balance sheets with ease, a feat I remain in awe of. After about an hour's discussion, in a situation that must be familiar to many, we both said yes because we found no reason to say no. We were married on the 10th of June, just three months after we first met. We are still happily together after 27 years and have a son Lalit, who was born in 1997.

I spent a year in CMC after returning from IIT. Sometime during that period, I saw an interesting ad for a job in Dubai. I applied to it and got it. It was with a heavy heart that I said goodbye to CMC after eight years. CMC remains the best place I have ever worked at, and the offices at Cuffe Parade, Bombay, hold some of my fondest memories of work and friendship.

The Dubai years

Sashi and I spent three years in Dubai, where I worked in the IT department of the National Bank of Dubai (NBD). Sashi got a job in accounts. To Indians venturing abroad for the first time, Dubai is a gentle introduction to the outside world. Many aspects of life are still familiar and there is a large expat Indian community there. At the same time, it is a multicultural work environment where you get to meet people from different nationalities and get used to international standards of working.

Professionally, I did well. I worked at NBD for three years and received two promotions during that period. But I found that, as I rose from a hands-on software developer to a project leader, the stress levels rose and I didn't enjoy the work as much.

Ultimately, I negotiated a more technical role for myself, working under a senior project leader who took on the more stressful management tasks. I only dealt with design and development issues.

That was a happy and exciting period for me, and I had learnt an important lesson too: Don't climb up the corporate ladder just because you are expected to. Your happiness and mental health are more important than 'career progress'.

Meanwhile, I hadn't forgotten my Australian dream. Two years after our arrival in Dubai, we re-applied to migrate to Australia. We were successful this time, because my M. Tech in computer science from IIT-K was recognised by the Australian immigration department, and I had also completed the required three years of post-qualification work experience.

My boss, the head of the IT department, told me when I was leaving, "If things don't work out, take the next flight back. There'll always be a place for you here." It was such heartwarming feedback, and I left Dubai with a warm glow.

The Australia years

We arrived in Australia in March 1998, with a few suitcases and a one-year-old child. From the point when I had first set foot in Singapore and had my mind blown, it had taken seven years to have my aspiration to live abroad realised.

My Dubai experience paid off immediately. At NBD, my team had developed the first internet home banking product in the Middle East using the then brand new Java technology. These skills were in hot demand in Australia; so I got a job with EDS Australia within a month of our arrival and was put to work on an internet corporate banking project for the Commonwealth Bank of Australia using Java.

I've since then changed a few jobs and gradually moved up the technical career ladder to become an IT architect. In spite of having a management degree, I avoided management positions at work and remained in a technical role, having learnt my lessons from the stressful time I had as a project leader in Dubai. I also learnt an important lesson about personal finances after moving to Australia.

I think I relaxed too quickly after migrating, thinking the journey was over, when it had only moved into a new phase. House prices in Sydney doubled in the five years after our arrival, and my failure to take the advice of family and friends to buy a house quickly proved costly.

Compound interest, as Einstein observed, is the eighth wonder of the world, and mistakes made with money also have a compounding effect. I reckon I could have retired comfortably by now had I invested in a house earlier, since every successive financial milestone took longer to achieve, but here we are. So here's a second lesson I would pass on to younger folks, which should temper my earlier advice to not place career progress above one's own happiness and mental health. Don't underestimate the importance of money in your life. The earlier you start to invest wisely and build your wealth, the happier you will be.

Today my son has also graduated, with a double degree in computer science and economics and is working as a data analyst with a company in Sydney. Sashi qualified herself with a CPA as soon as we arrived in Australia, since an Indian CA qualification was not recognised at the time, and she's been working with a government regulatory agency ever since.

As the only son of my parents, I have had the responsibility of taking care of them in their old age. Fortunately, the government of the then Prime Minister, John Howard, introduced what it called the Contributory Parent Migration visa, wherein the Australian government, on the basis of some actuarial calculations, charges a fee for parents' permanent residence visas, as advance payment for the burden they may impose in future on the Australian healthcare and social security systems. We willingly scraped together the money to pay for the visas of my parents, since otherwise we would have had to return to India as they got older. My father is unfortunately no longer with us, but my mother is part of our household, and life goes on.

I will be 60 in a couple of years. It has been a long and scenic journey from a green campus in Bangalore to a green suburb in Sydney, and every step of that journey has been enjoyable as well as educational.

Taking a Flight in Different Fields, In Different Countries

Abbas Raza Alvi

1971 admitted in B. Tech, IIT Kanpur, but proceeded to Moscow for M.Tech on a GOI scholarship.

> *Abbas Raza was educated in India, Russia and Australia. He is a poet, a writer, a speaker, a creative community networker and an entrepreneur. He is a strong advocate of protection of the environment and renewable energy.*
>
> *This is a story of an IITian who joined B. Tech in IIT Kharagpur due to his passion for aeroplanes and then left IIT Kharagpur to go to Russia on a fully-paid Government of India scholarship (including air fares). Then he came back to teach from where he left off. He currently lives in Sydney, Australia.*

Since my early childhood, I have had a particular attraction towards aircraft. I have always wanted to visit the airport and watch in fascination as the planes took off and landed.

My father worked throughout his life in railways and therefore, I had the privilege of travelling with my parents during my childhood in trains with free first-class passes. From my hometown, a tiny town, we used to travel to different parts of India, and during the number of journeys we have had, we used to come across the crossing of Kalyanpur railway station. IIT Kanpur's campus is located at Kalyanpur. In those days, I still remember that I used to request my parents to allow me to sit close to the train window to get a glimpse of IIT-K's airstrip and a little yellow glider aircraft just for a few seconds.

In my early school days, at a time when different types of engineering were beyond my comprehension, admission into IIT was a pathway to manufacturing aeroplanes and flying them. This dream of mine manifested itself into an extreme interest in pursuing admission to IIT Kanpur.

My one week at IIT Kanpur

After completing my 12th, intermediate school, I was announced as 'underage' and was not able to get admission to a number of good engineering institutions. Therefore, I joined the bachelor of science course at Aligarh Muslim University in 1969.

After completing B. Sc (honours) from AMU in 1971, I successfully completed the entrance examination of IIT. Financially, it was difficult for my family to allow me to study and live in an IIT hostel due to expenses. A deposit of the first instalment of Rs 341 in those days was high for a middle-income family. But it was arranged. I was interviewed and given admission in the first-year class of the five years integrated course in engineering degree. Words fail me as I try to describe the joyous moment of my life upon receiving my entrance examination results and my admission letter.

While I was just planning to move into the IIT-K hostel, I received a telegram from the Ministry of Education, India that I had been selected for free travel and scholarship to study turbo engineering in Moscow. The first flight of my life was an international flight to Moscow in 1971, and I realised my dream of flying and seeing an aircraft in motion, up close. I successfully finished my bachelor of engineering and master of engineering degrees in Moscow in 1977. But, under the agreement with the Government of India, I was required to return to India after my study and work for the government for one year. My first preference was to work in IIT Kanpur.

Yes, destiny had brought me back to IIT Kanpur again. I was interviewed by the head of the Department of Aeronautical Engineering, Prof C. S. Moorthy. I joined the Department of

Aeronautical Engineering at IIT Kanpur as a CSIR pool officer in 1977. I worked in the aeronautical engineering department for one year during 1977-1978 and then moved to the private sector corporations.

My engineering qualifications from Moscow have given me sound practical experience in engineering. My association and work in IIT Kanpur gave me the more theoretical experience of engineering, effective utilisation of computers as well as management skills. This unique combination helped me to build my career pathway.

I worked in India for 12 years, acquired more management qualifications and skills, and migrated to Australia in 1989. I had the opportunity to be the founding president of the Australia India Chamber of Commerce. For the last 32 years, I have been managing my own business and representing corporations for the marketing of their products and services in Australia.

My passion for IIT-K

For me, studying at IIT Kanpur was the dream of my childhood, but destiny gave me a unique opportunity to be a student for one week and then serve as the faculty for one year.

I still think that one day I may again visit IIT Kanpur and watch small aircraft flying on the airstrip.

Education in IIT Mumbai: Playing a Major Role in Facing Challenges

K. Ganga Raju

1966 Admitted in B.Tech Chemical Engineering,, IIT Mumbai but proceeded to Moscow on a GOI scholarship for M.Tech.

At the age of 10 years, I used to take our cattle to the grazing fields every Sunday. Sometime between 11 am and noon, an aeroplane used to fly over our agriculture fields. I wanted to fly in an aeroplane seeing this. That was my childhood dream.

My elder brother said that I should be good at English and mathematics to make my dream come true. So, I started getting up at 4 am every day to study. As there was no electricity in our small town, I had to study under the light of a hurricane lamp.

I used to read newspapers in my mother tongue (Telugu) up to SSLC. I joined B. Sc. in Andhra Loyola College. I went to the library every day to read the headlines in English newspapers. I also started maintaining a dairy for improving my English vocabulary. During the holidays at home, I started getting the *Times of India* daily newspaper by post (as there was no English newspaper circulation in the town at that time).

In 1966, after B. Sc graduation, I applied to a lateral entrance exam for IIT Bombay seeing an advertisement in the *Times of India*. I appeared for the entrance exam and viva-voce in Bombay and was selected for chemical engineering. I was one of the 14 selected candidates at that time.

Owing to the financial difficulties of our family, I applied for a Government of India Merit scholarship to go to Moscow (again after seeing an ad in the *Times of India*). Fortunately, I was selected in 1967 August; I was one of the candidates (out of 35 selected) from all over India.

I chose mining as my specialty (exploitation of hard mineral deposits, metal mining). The Government of India ensured employment after post-graduation, with a three-year contract agreement after returning from Moscow.

When I was doing B. Sc, I had purchased a book titled *How to Build a Better Vocabulary* by Maxwell Nurnberg and Morris Rosenblum for Rs 2, while travelling to Bombay. I had bought it at the Higginbotham's bookstore at the Pune railway station. This helped improve my English fluency and vocabulary. In my desire to be good at English, this was my companion, apart from Bhagavad Gita and the Bible for other reasons.

On returning from Moscow, I joined Hindustan Zinc Ltd (HZL), a public sector company then, in Rajasthan. RTZC of the UK were consultants to HZL. They found a big pool of highly skilled mining engineers in HZL, which they could tap into for their projects in Zambia (copper and cobalt). I was lucky to get selected. Zambia was a beautiful place to live in and the job was very rewarding. My luck later took me to jobs in Sultanate of Oman (Salalah BOT, setting up a cement plant), Saudi Arabia (cement plant, BOT), Mali (West Africa, cement plant, on BOT basis) and Cambodia (commissioning underground gold deposits). I retired as the country head in Cambodia. In all these projects, I was involved in training the workmen and junior executives of the respective countries and maintaining excellent working skills that matched international standards.

In India, I was associated with Coromandel Cements, Vishnu Cements and Anjani Cements, in setting up, commissioning and training subordinates and workers to reach international benchmarks.

I would like to mention here that I am fortunate to have worked in cement projects for seven years in Andhra Pradesh with Padma Sri and Padma Bhushan, B.V. Raju (former CMD of Cement Corporation of India, a Government of India undertaking), who established 12 cement projects in India.

I have 49 years of experience in setting up and commissioning of mining projects both in India and abroad.

I can say proudly that this is quite an achievement for a boy who was brought up in a village where there was no electricity and was rearing sheep.

At present, I am working as a freelance consultant for mining projects and as a guest faculty at some private engineering colleges to improve the standards of education in general. I have found that the standards of education have fallen very badly from the yester years that had five-star IITs. Improving the quality of education in my town is my passion now. This is what drives me and makes my life meaningful.

Life Between India and Australia

Ravi Gupta

1964- 1969 B. Tech Chemical engineering Vindyachal Hall; IIT Delhi

> *Ravi Gupta emigrated to Australia in 1981, and he has lived in Sydney for the past 40 years. He has run (and continues to run) numerous successful businesses and holds a large property portfolio. He is today among some of the richest Indians in Sydney. Ravi is a voracious reader and well-versed in current domestic and international politics and business affairs. Ravi's greatest joys in life are his family and cricket.*

Following B.Tech I did my M.Tech in Chemical Engineering followed by MBA from Delhi University, before joining National Industrial Development Corporation(NIDC). After some years with the NIDC and Bharat Heavy Electricals Ltd (BHEL), New Delhi, my real professional career started as a senior project engineer with EIL. I was involved in project planning and cost estimation for chemical, petrochemical and refinery projects. During my employment at EIL, the major achievement was my selection as project manager at a very high post with an amazing salary and perks.

The story goes like this. Abu Dhabi National Oil Company (ADNOC) conducted a global recruitment campaign to hire a few top talented engineers from around the globe and appointed Booz, Allen and Hamilton, a US based recruitment company for this.

All over India, only five people were selected for the interview to be held in Abu Dhabi. To my biggest surprise, I was one of the lucky ones who were selected for the interview. I was put up at the Hilton Abu Dhabi hotel for five days.

On the fourth day, I was surprised that I had still not been called for an interview. On Day 5, I got a call for interview. The interview panel comprised mostly Americans and British.

I did not know that my boss at EIL had also attended the same interview (for the same job). I got selected and that too at a much higher salary than my boss. When I met him in the office, we both tried to keep it confidential. Finally, we openly talked about the interview.

Also, while at EIL, I got another offer as deputy manager from Zambi Copper Mines. In the end, I did not take either of the two offers as I had already applied for migration to Australia.

Migration to Australia

I migrated to Australia in 1981, with no pre-arranged job. At that time, most people in India did not know much about Australia. Even my late father, who was himself highly educated, told me that I was making a mistake leaving such a good job and going to a land where there were only kangaroos and jungles and where people played only cricket all day.

My wife was employed as the head of department for mathematics at Delhi University College and could not leave her job; so, I had to come alone.

I resigned from my job at EIL and asked the personnel department if they could give me the names of some Indians from the computer engineering department who had migrated to Australia. I was given a short list of names. Before leaving India, I wrote to them explaining my situation and that I was travelling to Australia hoping to find someone who could help me settle in a foreign country. No one wrote back.

Before leaving India, I was informed by the Australian High Commission in New Delhi that, upon my arrival in Sydney, I would be provided accommodation at a migrant hostel and a local guide. To my biggest surprise, when I landed in Sydney that afternoon, there was no local guide and no accommodation. I was told that the migrant hostel accommodation was for European migrants and not for Indians. I started to panic.

To my surprise and by the grace of God, I was greeted at the airport by an Indian computer professional to whom I had written prior to leaving India. I had never met this man before in my life, but he took me to his house and I stayed with him for a week. After one week, I moved to YMCA, before befriending another Indian IIT fellow, who allowed me to stay with him and his family. To this day, I owe both these men a debt of gratitude. I will never forget the kindness they showed me in my time of need.

I got a job in two weeks with an American company as a senior applications engineer for chemical and mining projects. I was offered a higher salary than most of the computer professional working in Sydney, which was quite a surprise to me and my friends.

After some time, I rented a one-bedroom apartment and asked my wife to join me as I had a place to stay and a job. My wife came to Australia after taking a five-year study leave for Ph.D. Her plan initially was to stay for five years before returning to India to join her work again.

Next we moved into a two-bedroom flat in West Ryde. One weekend afternoon. we were looking for a unit to buy. We were browsing through the *Sydney Morning Herald* newspaper. Although we had no money, we went to a real estate agent anyway, found a small place in North Ryde that we liked, and secured the property with a $20-holding deposit.

In 1986, my son was born. My wife moved back to India to join her job, as her five-year leave was over. After a few months, I resigned from my job and moved back to India.

We took transfer of residence (called 'TR'), booked a container and took everything to India, including our three-year-old Mazda 626 basic model car.

Moving back to India

I was really worried that I wouldn't be able to get a job in India as I had been out of touch for so many years. Luckily, I got a job with Kanoria Chemical Industries as vice-president of new projects at the company's office in Vasant Vihar, New Delhi.

My job involved identification and implementation of new projects, technology transfer, licensing and coordination.

As part of my role at Kanoria Chemical Industries, I was sent on a business trip to the USA and Europe on several occasions, which was a rare practice at that time. The world has changed significantly now. I do remember my very first trip to America vividly. Due to my transfer of residence, I nearly didn't make it on the plane. At the last minute, I had to call the chief customs officer at Delhi airport and explain the urgency of my situation. Fortunately, I made it!

After a few years, I was offered a position at Prakash Industries Lt, Rajendra Place, New Delhi as the general manage and the head of the video tape division. Back in those days, the VCR was in great demand and Prakash Industries was a leading manufacturer of blank video tapes. The plant was located in Kashipur in UP and employed around 200 people.

One of the obstacles I had to overcome as part of my new role involved the solvent

that the plant was using. When I started the job, the company was importing the solvent from overseas, which was quite an expensive proposition, costing a lot of foreign exchange. In order to help the organisation save money, I designed a solvent recovery system, whereby the solvent vapours were recycled so that they could be reused. As a result, my solvent recovery system was replicated and later used by J.K. Chemicals India.

During my time at Prakash Industries, I visited a number of countries in Europe and North America in order to find the most efficient and advanced technology for use in our plant. On one of my first trips to England, after the technical discussions were over, I received a special invitation for dinner. To my surprise, I was greeted by the company's managing director and his wife who had booked a lavish Indian restaurant for our meal together. During the discussion, the MD offered me a kickback, in return for my recommendation of his technology to use in our plant back in India. He tried to suggest that he knew the Indian system very well and that this was how things were done in India. I was appalled at this proposition. I told him that I would only be recommending technology to our plant in India based on merit and nothing else; I would not compromise my integrity.

Sadly, this was just the first of the several instances in which people attempted to offer kickbacks or bribes to strike a deal. Over time, it created a certain level of frustration with the Indian business culture. It was demoralising and emotionally fatiguing. After three years, although I had a great job, salary, a company car and a driver, I made the decision to move back to Australia. When I broke the news to my wife, she was understandably confused and upset by my decision to leave our good life behind. However, I reassured her that we would be okay even though deep down I too had similar fears. Nevertheless, we decided to move back to Australia together.

Moving back to Australia

After working in corporate organisations for a few years in Australia, I wanted control over my life, which comes with running one's own business. After looking at a few options, I came across a franchise opportunity for a Shell Australia service station. My wife was apprehensive as we had never run our own business before and we would be leaving behind the comfort and certainty of a regular salary. But I submitted the application to see if I could get the job. By the grace of God, I managed to secure the franchise, despite significant competition.

Working in my own business was an eye-opening experience. I realised that, with efficient management, hard work and innovation there was no limit to one's success. This was demonstrated through my contribution to the Shell network in Australia, when my cost reduction recommendations were implemented in the Shell service stations across the country.

After getting a taste for small business, I went on to build my own childcare centre. Then I acquired another childcare centre and also operated a post office.

Throughout my time as a small business owner, I have endeavoured to give opportunities to young Indians who have migrated to Australia—in the same way a stranger once picked me up from Sydney airport without knowing who I was.

To be honest, it is hard to summarise 40 years in 4 pages.

Most IIT graduates think that IIT will give them a passport to success. However, that is not always the case. I believe that, to be successful in life, one has to be honest, compassionate and hardworking and have clear goals and perseverance in life. My key advice to anyone reading this would be to take risks and follow the courage of your convictions. We are all human beings; it is okay to fail but sometimes risks pay off in ways that we cannot imagine. I firmly believe it is not about what I have gained but about the person I have become.

My greatest achievement is having a loving family. I live in Sydney with my wife, son, daughter-in-law and our adorable puppy. My wife and I are both retired, while my son is a consultant ophthalmologist.

The Patelian Way

Raghu Puri

1977-1982-86, B. Tech -Chemical Engineering, Patel Hall, IIT Kharagpur

Raghu Puri is from Patel Hall (batch of 1982-86). He is a former VP of Cisco Systems USA and is currently a CEO of a multinational firm. He successfully started and sold a start-up in the USA. This gave him financial security for the rest of his life and the freedom to do what he likes to do. While his parents gave him values in his early years, his four years at IIT Kharagpur gave him the foundation for the rest of his life. At IIT, he developed the confidence to do anything, learnt business management and fiscal responsibility through campus projects, and acquired leadership skills through student representation at IIT Senate. Relationships forged in Patel Hall stood as support during a traumatic personal event and became the catalyst of a fortuitous opportunity that propelled him to the US. These bonds have prevailed over the past 30 years of his career spanning global leadership roles across Sprint, Cisco and Accenture. Strengthened through social media, these relationships provided an opportunity to organise support globally to give back to IIT and Patel Hall.

My journey to adulthood began when I joined IIT Kharagpur in August 1982. I was allocated accommodation at the Patel Hall of Residence, which has the distinction of being the first hostel of the first IIT. I arrived just two days after the mass event of 'getting to know each other'. While my parents have been my life guides, who gave me my values, my four years at IIT Kharagpur gave me the foundation for the rest of my life. Patel Hall and its residents, affectionately known as 'Basti', were core to my development, which has helped me over the past 35 years of my professional and personal life.

Since my father was an executive in the Indian Railways and Kharagpur was a key division with the 'longest railway platform', I showed up with some unwanted buzz, as there was an entourage of junior railway staff accompanying my father. The buzz also drew attention to the various badminton racquets that arrived with me. Within two hours, I was accosted by Suresh Rajgopal, Small Area Games Secretary, who enrolled me in the 'Fresher Games' for badminton, boxing, weightlifting and anything else I was willing to 'volunteer' for. This was my first brush with the 'you can do anything' attitude, which went a long way in building my confidence for future endeavours. It also set me up with some level of recognition as I turned out to be one of the better badminton players. I was always at the centre of activity in the Technology Gymkhana for the next four years.

While I missed the informal orientation, over the next few years I did not miss out on any opportunity to build strong and lifelong relationships. As Kharagpur was so far away from any city, it was necessary to be with friends 24X7 and they eventually became family. We had no social media to distract us, nor did we have too many entertainment choices, except for some programmes on TV and some music over the radio in the common room, which we competed to control. Our entertainment was a combination of institutional events—sports, dramatics, music, etc. These were in the form of inter-hall events where the spirit of the hall and the support for the same prevailed over any talent we could bring to the forum. Team spirit and the quality of working together for the good of the larger body were developed through these events. In some events, we would be on the team, but in other instances we were willing cheerleaders who stood by the sidelines, shouting hoarse in support of our team's success.

The more personal form of entertainment was the long *bhaat* sessions that went well into the wee hours of the morning. We would talk on every subject under the sun. We did not have the privilege of Google search, but we did not lack in opinions. We were forced to use logic, interpretation, point and counter-point to drive an agreement, aligned with our objective. Our discussions started from the post-dinner gathering outside the mess, continued to the connecting balustrades within our blocks, and culminated in the canteen, between copious cups of tea and snacks. We met various philosophers on every subject. With effective listening, we developed knowledge of whom to go to for what expertise—a handy tool that has served me well whenever I switched roles throughout my career. We also learned to look beyond accent or manner of delivery, since we had people from all over the country, and we looked only at the essence of the content. This training helped me in the various global roles I had in my career, wherein I managed people from all over the world, including the five-year stint I had based out of Shanghai, China, when I managed the infrastructure business for Cisco in Asia-Pacific.

Student elections were another factor in our young lives, forcing an articulation of our vision to secure broad support for the elected positions within the hall or across IIT. I had the privilege of being elected the secretary of Small Area Games during my second year. During that period, we conceived a key project to convert the empty land between Patel, Nehru and Azad Halls into a basketball court. This entailed securing funds from not just Patel Hall but also from the other halls. The budget general body meeting of a hall was an experience few people can forget. The debates on spending, with demand for detailed justification, would have put to shame even the most vibrant democratic debates of the Pnyx in Athens.

I had the challenge of not only running the gauntlet of Patel Hall's general body meetings but also that of the other halls to secure a total funding of Rs 15,000, which today would amount to Rs 2 lakh, taking into consideration the impact of inflation. With support from a few advocates in each hall, we were able to bag the funding. Then began the challenge of negotiating with contractors and managing the construction and inauguration with the requisite institute political hierarchy–Director, President Gymkhana as well as campus leaders. This experience helped me develop skills in business proposals, fiscal responsibility and project coordination and culminated in a decision to switch over from engineering to business as a career choice.

The elections became more complicated when running for higher leadership roles like the vice-president of the Gymkhana, who was the directly elected student leader of IIT. In addition, this person would be the lead student representative in the IIT Senate, the governing body of the institute. In my first year, we backed the winning candidate from Azad, but in my second year we backed a candidate from Patel who lost. In our third year, we supported a Patel Hall candidate, Arjun Sen, who won the VP position. These campaigns required the coordination of supporters across various halls, who were advocates and brought out the votes on election day. The cumulative effort of networking across three different campaigns positioned me well for the secondary election for the undergraduate student representative to the IIT Senate. This was an electoral college vote by the presidents of the undergraduate student halls. Thanks to my prior engagements and relationships, I won the election. After a very long time, both the student representatives to the IIT Senate were from Patel Hall. This experience in student leadership and my ability to impact policy reinforced my interest in management. I was trained early at IIT for various leadership positions in my career and this training enabled me to engage across functional leadership to build consensus and present effectively in the C-Suite.

The relationships we forged within Patel Hall were akin to that of an expanded family that was with us in times of joy and more so in times of need. I recall a time when I was hospitalised with a bad case of bronchitis at B. C. Roy Hospital for a few days. I had a constant stream of visitors, from my wing, my batch, seniors and juniors.

This happened to any Patelian, who had the unfortunate experience of being admitted to a hospital.

The most moving representation of this bond was evident in a defining moment in my young life, when my father suddenly passed away during my second semester. I rushed from Kharagpur to Calcutta early in the morning to be with my family and be there for my father's last rites. Later that day, on coming back from the hospital, I was stunned to see over 20 Patelians at my house. They had come to give me their support, the kind one can get only from brothers. Till date, my eyes tear up and I have a catch in my throat whenever I recall their quiet presence at the prayer ceremony.

These relationships have continued over the years wherein Patelians go out of their way to host one another during a visit of either a family member or Patelian's child in college. They also offer their support for professional connections. Building and retaining such professional and personal networks have become critical to my career success.

A prime example of value from these relationships forms another defining moment in my life. In my final year at IIT, I decided to pursue a career in business. I was one of the very few people on campus who had taken the GMAT in addition to the GRE. Fortuitously, in December that year, Dr. Probir Roy, a professor of finance had come to the campus to present a paper at the Department of Architecture, on behalf of his sibling in the US. During a hosted lunch with IIT students, he mentioned that he was looking for graduate research assistants in his MBA programme. One of my wing mates, Ashok Malhotra, happened to be at the luncheon and he told Dr. Roy that he had a candidate who had already taken the GMAT. Ashok came back to the hall to take me to the professor, but I was not in the hall. All my wing mates rallied together and started looking for me at the usual haunts across the 2000-acre campus. That day, I had gone to Kharagpur town to meet my local host family for dinner. When I came back at 1 am in the morning, my wing mates and many of the Patelians in the hall were waiting to curse me for missing a golden opportunity.

Later that morning, I met Dr. Roy as he walked from his place of residence to the mess for breakfast. During that 15-minute walk, he offered me a scholarship while I worked for him as a research assistant. Given the loss of my father early in life, the only way I could have dreamed to study in the US was through sponsorship. A combination of my Patelian brothers' tenacity, a mentor in Dr. Roy, and providence set me on a journey of success.

Over the past 35 years I have had the privilege of holding leadership positions at Sprint, Scientific-Atlanta/Cisco, Accenture and DXC, where I have had global roles and managed a portfolio in excess of $1billion. Throughout my career, I have not hesitated to take risks whenever opportunity knocked, since I had experienced success very early.

I took a risk and moved my family across the world to Shanghai, China, on an expatriate assignment with Cisco. We lived and worked here for five years. In addition to being a great career move, it also gave me the opportunity to expose my children to a new culture and a new language, which they still speak fluently. This has helped them in their college and career progression.

Using WhatsApp as a tool, we Patelians have created many 'Basti' subnets that allow us to rekindle the best experience of our lives. Using these networks, we have hosted over five reunions in the US, with over 25 attendees from all over the world. Similarly, other groups have hosted reunions in India with over 100 attendees. These are great opportunities to reconnect with friends and form a bridge across other Patelians, beyond our four-year connection at Patel Hall.

The biggest power of these alumni networks is the ability to mobilise in order to give back. Thanks to a vision conceived at our 25th reunion, when we had the largest number of people from a batch, we asked the president what we could do for the hall. Based on his request, we created a fund drive which, within a week, raised over Rs 1 crore (US$150,000). With the strong leadership of the Patelian team in India, we rebuilt the mess kitchen with contemporary equipment, revamped the mess seating area, and completely redid the common room. The strength of the Patelians was also evident in the recent Covid-19 crisis, wherein, within the span of a week, the Patelian team raised over 3.5 lakh (US$50,000) to alleviate the oxygen crisis via donations. We also continue to support mess workers at Patel Hall through donations to their families and sponsorship of education opportunities for their children.

Though many of us are living in various parts of the world, we can trace back our professional success to many lessons learnt at Patel Hall and IIT Kharagpur. The ties of being a Patelian bind us, regardless of the location or the year in which we graduated. This gives us an automatic entry into a club that is always welcoming and supporting through any crisis or celebration in our lives. It is a privilege to be a Patelian and I count myself lucky to not just belong to this group but also, in a small way, contribute to the fabric of the Patelian ethos.

I successfully started and sold a start-up in the USA. That gave me financial security for the rest of my life and empowered me to do what I like to do in life.

Once a Patelian, always a Patelian for life!

ISRO and Dr. A.P.J. Abdul Kalam

Dr. Srikant Bandyopadhyay

1966-1971 B.Tech Metallurgy IIT Kharagpur

Srikanta Bandyopadhyay did a two-year M. Tech course in materials science, after taking an official leave from his position at ISRO/SSTC Trivandrum, Department of Materials and Quality Control. The M. Tech course at IIT Kanpur helped him proceed in his career and specialise in composites, nanomaterials and recycling technology.

He is an avid singer and a music composer, for which he has received many appreciation letters, including one from IIT Kharagpur.

I am a 'double IITian', having done my B. Tech from IIT Kharagpur and M. Tech from IIT Kanpur. For me, transition from IIT Kharagpur to IIT Kanpur was easy as I was already an IITian.

I was in IIT Kanpur's first batch of M. Tech in materials science, set up in 1971 by IIT Kanpur's Professor E. C. Subbarao (metallurgical engineering) and co-supported by Prof C. N. R. Rao (chemistry), Prof D. Chakravorty (metallurgy), Prof P. N. Murthy (aero engineering), and several other IIT Kanpur academics from physics, civil engineering, mechanical engineering, and so on.

I did my M. Tech thesis at IIT Kanpur on glass fibre reinforced polymer composites, supervised by Prof P. N. Murthy. The thesis generated an international refereed journal paper—S. Bandyopadhyay and Murthy, P.N. (1975) 'Experimental Studies on Interfacial shear Strength in Glass Fibre Reinforced Plastics Systems', Materials Science and Engineering, Vol. 19, pp. 139-145.

IIT Kanpur was an excellent institution where I developed in-depth knowledge in all parts of science and engineering. When I completed my M. Tech degree and returned to employment at ISRO/ SSTC Trivandrum, my background was utilised by Dr. A. P. J. Abdul Kalam, rocket technology leader, through his composites technology team, including Mr C. R. Sathya and others.

When Dr. Kalam later became the President of India, he still remembered me. Upon being approached by me from UNSW, Sydney, President Kalam invited me to the Presidential Palace in July 2004. That meeting subsequently resulted in the AISRF Project Scheme between Australia and India, amounting to $50 million, which started around 2009 and is still going on. I was given a top-down project on 'Nanocomposites in Clean Energy', involving six Australian academics and six Indian academics including IACS researchers. I was given A$1.55 million for this project.

In 2010, I was selected as one of the chairmen of the IIT Kanpur Golden Jubilee Celebration event.

In 2018, I was selected by the Indian government's GIAN committee to give lectures for one week (20 hours) at IIT Kanpur on novel fly ash technology.

For more information, visit these websites of the event organised by Prof K. K. Kar of IIT Kanpur.

http://www.gian.iitkgp.ac.in//files/brochures/ BR1511759651Prof_Kamal_K_Kar_Brochure.pdf

My YouTube GIAN lectures at IIT Kanpur in 2018

https://www.youtube.com/watch?v=KU8inqL4nrkandlist= PL48UwQJyfW3SyKO6K9jf3QCBa8cN8A177

I was the Scientist of the Year in 1984 at Aus Defence DSTOMRL, Melbourne and one of the Top 5 Inventors, selected by Campus Review Australia 2013.

I have co-authored/co-edited three engineering books.

1. A Srinivasan and S Bandyopadhyay, Editors: Advances in Polymer Materials and Technology by CRC Press/Taylor and Francis Group (2016), ISBN 9781498718813 - CAT# K25469; July 11, 2016 by CRC Press Reference - 808 Pages - https://doi.org/10.1201/9781315371054

2. A Hauptstein, S Bandyopadhyay, D Lambino: E-beam Deformation of Ceramic Particles – The Effects of Electron Irradiation on Morphology, Modification and Microstructure of Talc Powder; LAP Lambert Academic Publishing Germany, ISBN 978-3-8454-1828-5; 292 pages, 04 August 2011

3. D Nath and S Bandyopadhyay: High Strength Polymer Fly Ash Composites – Fundamental Understanding, Lambert Academic Publishing Germany, 2011, ISBN: 978-3-8465-1146-6

The Rollercoaster Journey of Music and Engineering

Rameshwar K. Maini

1962-67, B.Tech, Civil Engineering, IIT Bombay

Rameshwar Mani left home as a 16-year-old boy, entered IIT-Bombay and came out a man. From facing trials and tribulations due to his desire to become a successful singer, in a day and age when finding piles of money on the street was more likely than making it big in the music industry, to becoming a successful businessman, who is the CEO of his own engineering firm, Rameshwar's life is the stuff of dreams. He persevered all through his life. His company Zentech recently, in partnership with Blue Whale Ocean Filtration, developed vessels that are specifically designed for removal of microplastics from lakes, rivers and oceans.

I was born in 1946 in Ludhiana, Punjab. My first love was singing. I was one of 11 in the school music team that went to different towns in Punjab and sang during major functions, including national holidays such as Independence Day, or when Indira Gandhi visited Ludhiana.

We sat in front of Indira Gandhi and sang patriotic songs, written and produced by our school music teacher, who was a musical genius. We earned money for the school by singing around town and spent most of our school days practising new songs that our music teacher produced with his own music.

Somewhere in 1961, during the last year of my higher secondary certification, I became serious about my studies, thought I cannot fathom the reason for that change in me. The results of my hard work put me in the elite list of top students in the Punjab higher secondary school exams. That was the first year when higher secondary students could take up the IIT entrance exam. I decided to appear for the exam, though our school teachers wanted us to join ITT so that we could become good welders and technicians.

My brilliant sister, who was a mathematics professor, gave me a crash course for two months to learn higher level mathematics. But I was sure that I would not clear the entrance exam.

It was a Sunday, the last day for receiving the selection letter from IIT. I concluded that I had definitely failed in the exam. I was sleeping in the day when my sister woke me up and told me that a special delivery letter had come, declaring my selection to IIT. I was to appear for an interview in Kanpur. (IIT Delhi did not exist in 1962.)

Since I was sure that I was never going to be selected for IIT, I had torn my IIT entrance exam pass to save the photo for an application to another university. Since I had mutilated the pass, which was required for the interview, I was afraid that I had lost the golden opportunity. A friend in the neighbourhood, who was an IITian, told me not to worry about it and go for my interview. The rest, as they say, was history.

As I loved music, I chose IIT Bombay for further studies. I thought I would get a taste of the music industry, which consisted of stalwarts like Mohamed Rafi and Lata Mangeshkar. I had heard that Bombay was a beautiful city and I was excited to go to Bombay.

My parents were not educated. My father had studied up to the fourth grade and my dear mother had no education. My father put me on a train to Bombay and asked one of the young men in the bogie that I was riding in to help me on the way. I was just 16 years of age then.

The next morning, I was up in the early hours. The train took two days to reach Bombay. It entered Kalyan early in the morning and I could see only filth on either side of the track. I was totally shattered to see this. The buildings looked shabby, as though they had never been painted. It was a real shock for someone who was expecting clean roads and buildings. The young man, whom my father had requested to help me, had changed his ticket from Kalyan to Bombay VT. He told me that he had friends in the film industry and that we could put our luggage in a storage space at VT station, so that he could introduce me to his friends from the film industry. I don't know why, but I decided to get down in Dadar, which came after the university station of Vikhroli. I felt that the young man was not trustworthy. He insisted that I should not get down at Dadar but I did. I hired a coolie to take my luggage to the train going to Vikhroli station. I had no prior experience in travelling, but God must have been directing me. I was going to IIT for the first time and I had nine pieces of luggage with me, including a tall earthen neck pitcher called *surahi* in Punjabi! The coolie put all my luggage in the train at Dadar but at Vikhroli I had to pull out all nine pieces of luggage by myself to get off the train, which stopped for less than a minute. I threw the *surahi* on the train tracks and reduced my load to eight pieces.

I somehow dragged all my luggage out of the train station and waited for the university bus. It was around 6:30 am and raining hard. Right outside the station was a restaurant, which was closed at that moment. All the employees were sitting outside, almost naked, with their bellies hanging about. I was afraid. It seemed as though one of them would kill me soon. I was alone at the bus stop and had no idea when the next bus would come.

Eventually, the university bus came and I boarded it with all my luggage. The bus dropped me at the main campus. I tried to find my hostel, but I could not find my name. My last name was written as 'Naini' instead of 'Maini'. Someone told me to go to hostel #4, where there was someone from my hometown of Ludhiana. I asked a porter to help me. We both walked to hostel #4. At the reception, someone called for my senior from Ludhiana. He came there and started to rag me. Somehow I found out that I was assigned to the brand new hostel #6. I asked the porter to help me to walk up to hostel #6. It was raining hard and we both walked through the rain to reach the hostel. Since it was a new hostel, there was no one to rag me. Though I felt good, I cried a lot that day.

University started in the first week of July. We students would walk to the main campus. We could see the rain coming when we went past Powai Lake. We would run at full speed to take cover inside the gymnasium on the way to the main campus or just reach the camps somehow. However, we would be totally wet by the time we reached the campus. We would attend classes sitting in wet clothes, during the months of July and August. We did not have washers and dryers in those days. We would wash our clothes and dry them in our own rooms. Sometimes we would wear wet clothes too. It wasn't fun. But we did have the luxury of private rooms even though the wall between two rooms would not reach all the way to the top. We could talk to our next-door neighbour through the exposed top part of the wall, without seeing each other. I became an entertainer in my wing by singing songs in the evenings.

The year I had joined IIT Bombay, there was a rule called 'RB7'. If we failed in the first year, we would be sent back home. We were all worried about this and were ragged by our seniors, who said that we "idiots and lazy bums" would be sent home because we were not very smart. I was always worried about this rule. I worried that, if I was sent home, my family would think I had goofed off instead of studying. I studied really hard but I was still languishing at the bottom of the class, until the third year when I came first in my class.

During my first year in IIT, I was always the last one to finish writing the exams. Others would submit their papers in a very short duration, while I would be grinding through the allotted time period, till the very end. Later I learned that all the smart guys who finished their exams quickly had completed B. Sc before coming to IIT. I had come straight from higher secondary school. I had never studied these subjects, which the others had completed in their B. Sc courses. The experience was painful.

In my second year, I became a singer at the university and a long-distance runner as well. I ran the 1500-m and 5000-m races regularly. I would win the 1500-m races but I was always second in the 5000-m races. I would practise running 12 to 15 laps every day. I later became a part of the relay team and ran all relay races from 100 m to 5000m. I did win a number of medals in the various races. I became the monitor of my hostel too. I also participated in the election for the post of the music secretary of the university. But I lost the election. There were a number of silly comments on my posters that read 'Maini for M and Maini for Music'.

At the start of my second year, my father asked me if I would delay my trip to IIT because my sister was to be married in the first week of July. My father, or for that matter no one in my family, had never asked for my opinion in any matter. This was the first time. I felt I must have arrived in life for my father, of all people, was asking me for my presence at my sister's wedding!

But I wasn't going to miss the first few days of my second year, though I was still reeling from the tough first year of schooling. I told my father that I couldn't delay my trip to IIT. For my benefit, my father moved my sister's wedding two weeks in advance and I participated in my sister's wedding.

Overall, my five years in IIT Bombay gave me a lot of confidence for life. The traits of hard work and honesty and the ability to rise up to any challenge, without being left behind, came from my days in IIT. The credit for whatever I am today must go to my sister, who taught me mathematics before my IIT entrance exam, my years at IIT, and my brilliant friends whom I had met in this glorious institution.

I came to the USA in 1967 to join Berkeley, but the university wouldn't give any scholarship for the first year. Then I decided to seek admission in Canada at the University of British Columbia, Vancouver. I got admission and scholarship at this university. I finished my masters' degree course in structural engineering in less than a year and worked in an engineering company in Vancouver for one year. Then I moved to New York to work for an engineering company, which was a pioneer in finite element analysis. My thesis professor during my master's course was the VP of this company. One year later, I was sent to Los Angeles to run an office there. But a month-and-a-half later, I was moved to Europe to run the company's office there. I stayed in the Netherlands (then it was Holland) for one-and-a-half years, travelling all over Europe for my company. I was then moved to London to run the company's office there.

I got sick and tired of moving. I told my company that I wanted to come back to the US. The company was opening an office in Houston and I was asked to run that office. Before coming to Houston, I went home and got married within seven days. I got my wife her passport within two weeks and applied for her visa to the US. She joined me in Houston in less than two months as a US immigrant on green card. I am writing this to tell you how easy it used to be to become an immigrant to the US in 1972.

In 1969, I became a US immigrant in less than three months and was ready to go to Vietnam to fight in the war. It was compulsory to go to Vietnam in those days. I was fortunate that I didn't get drafted, while many of my friends in my neighbourhood in New York were running away to Canada to avoid the draft.

I came to Houston, Texas from Europe in 1972. I did spend three years in Europe (1975-1978) building and moving drilling rigs offshore in the North Sea. When we moved to France in 1975, my wife was seven months pregnant. Our first child was born in Paris, France. In 1978, when we came back to the US, my wife was expecting our second child, who was born in Houston. I have been living in Houston for the last 49 years.

In 1977, while we were still in Europe, I started an engineering company with two American business partners. The three of us moved to Houston in 1978. I have been running the same business, supporting engineering projects all around the world in the offshore drilling industry, including some bridges in the USA. We have also worked for NASA, US Airforce and US Maritime Administration.

I am truly blessed with a strong team of professionals across our offices in various countries, including India, UAE, Brazil, Mexico and Malaysia. Our head office is in Houston, Texas.

Recently, Zentech, our company, in partnership with Blue Whale Ocean Filtration, developed vessels that are specifically designed for removal of microplastics from lakes, rivers and oceans. When aquatic life, fish and other marine animals consume plastic waste, the waste accumulates inside their GI tracts, which can cause physical harm to them. Plastic also leaches toxic chemical contaminants such as PFAS, PFOA and TOC into fish and marine life and into the ocean environment. The contaminated fish often ends up being served in restaurants and in the homes of people around the world. This project is my passion with the objective of giving back to society.

I thank IIT for my great life and for many of the smart people I have had the privilege of meeting in this life.

The Poetry of Engineering

Sundaram 'Sundy' Srinivasan

1979-1984, B.Tech, Mechanical Engineering, Jwalamukhi Hall, IIT Delhi

Sundaram Srinivasan is the COO of Zentich Inc, in the USA. He has been actively involved in the activities of the IIT alumni for close to 20 years. He was the Founding President of IIT Alumni of Greater Houston (IITAGH). He has also held the position of President, PanIIT USA.

His poetry has been published in a few anthologies. He also does stand-up comedy as a hobby; he has performed stand-up comedy at many PanIIT conferences.

My story is as intricate as the story of an IITian can be. My dad was with the Post and Telegraph Department, GOI, which took me to various parts of India, wherever he was posted. I have studied in eight schools in different states through my 12 years of high school—as far west as Rajasthan, as far north as Delhi, as far south as Bangalore and as far east as Assam. This meant that I was brought up to be truly 'Indian' in every sense of the word and I got accepted easily into almost every group.

I can blend in among a group of Bengalis and a group of Punjabis just as easily as I can among a group of Tamilian friends. I get accepted easily. I am privileged to have experienced this as a result of living across various parts of the country. I was also brought up by my dad with the freedom to eat, drink or do almost anything that I liked (although I am a Tamil Brahmin). He encouraged me to experience life and this stood me in good stead both at IIT and in the world beyond.

These aspects made my life quite enjoyable at IIT Delhi. IIT was a different experience—after being among the top three students in my class in school, I had to rapidly adjust to being just mediocre at IIT.

I had to find my niche and grab the opportunity that IIT gave me to do the things I was passionate about. I represented IIT-D in elocutions competitions, debates and Just a Minute sessions. Thus, I was able to improve my skills in public speaking.

I made lifelong friends in IIT-D and enjoyed life, not bothering about studies too much. I have always believed that almost anyone who has got into IIT can score well academically, if they really put their mind to it. Unfortunately, focusing only on studies means one has to sacrifice all other aspects of the incredible mosaic that IIT offers to develop one's personality.

It so happened that a friend once challenged me to prove my theory and get 10 points out of 10. This, of course, meant studying all the time and doing nothing else. I did that and managed to win the bet. Soon after, I was back to my life as a 'vela' (a Punjabi word meaning 'a person with nothing to do') in IIT-D. IIT-D gave me the ticket to life. I passed out from IIT-D in 1984 and was picked up on campus by Godfrey Phillips.

It so happened that, after six months of passing out, I went back to campus to have drinks with my friends only to find out that Schlumberger of the US was coming for campus interviews. It was a highly lucrative opportunity as the company offered an international career. I was extremely lucky to be selected and posted in France.

Dame Fortune has truly smiled on me. Here is a simple example of that. In those days, overseas travel and the French visa were very difficult to get. It so happened that, at that time, the French Ambassador to India was caught up in a spy scandal. Therefore, to appease India and Indians, the French Embassy quickly issued visas to applicants. I was lucky to get the French visa quickly, despite a half-baked application. The air ticket to France now posed a problem, as air tickets were very expensive those days and there was no way my father could afford to buy one for me. Here again, my luck factor kicked in. A secretary dealing with my case, Elvina D'Souza in Schlumberger, was instrumental in getting me a paid ticket from Schlumberger in France. Had it not been for her, who knows where I might be today! I will forever be grateful to her for sincerely helping a young kid make his career.

In my work of over 25 years with this company, I have had the opportunity to live in many countries across all continents, other than Antarctica. I thoroughly enjoyed this.

Midlife crisis set in midway through my Schlumberger career and I wanted to do something different. At the age of about 40, I applied for an MBA in MIT USA and luckily I was accepted. Schlumberger gave me study leave on the condition that, after my MBA, I would come back and join the company. This I did.

Later I quit Schlumberger to join BP. Then I actually went back to Schlumberger again for a few years. In 2013, at one of the events of IIT Alumni of Greater Houston, I happened to bump into the CEO of Zentech, Ramesh Maini, an IIT-B alumnus. This was one of the best things that happened to me. For the last seven years, I have been working for Zentech in Houston, Texas, USA.

How I became the president of PanIIT USA is a story I would like to tell. In 2003, I attended Pravasi Bharatiya Divas in Delhi. There I got an opportunity to meet the former President of India, Dr. Abdul Kalam, over a cup of tea at Rashtrapati Bhavan. I went in with the usual attitude of an NRI and an IITian. However, I came out a very different person. I was greatly influenced by the president. I was told that the best I could do for India was to be a good ambassador for my motherland and contribute to the community I lived and work in. This singular thought has influenced me deeply and I owe it to President Kalam for truly opening my mind to this pure, simple but extremely important concept.

I was on a mission now. On my return to Houston, I got involved with a great team and set up IITAGH (Houston Chapter of PanIIT USA) and got it registered as a 501 c3 charitable organisation. I started helping with PanIIT conferences. I

found that PanIIT USA comprised some wonderful people but there was also a dark side to it. In general, many people I met had inflated egos and lacked the right spirit for truly and effectively showcasing the wonders of the IIT. I was quite vocal and critical about this, and unfortunately I rubbed many people the wrong way. Rajat Gupta and Witty Bindra, with their wisdom and vision, then on the board of PanIIT USA, asked me to come in as the president of PanIIT USA. They gave me the opportunity to implement my ideas, a proposition I could not turn down. After meeting President Abdul Kalam, I had developed a strong desire to contribute to my community and be a good ambassador of India. It is to Rajat and Witty that I owe my gratitude for providing me a broader platform to work from.

When I was working in France, I learned something interesting about the French Foreign Legion. They were the toughest and most feared regiment in France and hence the most prestigious. However, they comprised mostly migrants of non-French origin e.g., Moroccans, Algerians and other North Africans. The French president was once asked to comment on the Foreign Legion. He is said to have remarked, "They are truly French, NOT because of the blood they HAVE but because of the blood they GAVE." I realised that, to be sincere to any cause, for instance PanIIT, it is not only important to have its blood flowing in you but you must also give your blood for it and truly appreciate those who do so. It does not matter if someone is young or new, if someone contributes to something, they must be recognised to the hilt. So, it is with this spirit that I ran IITAGH and run PanIIT now and I hope this spirit will continue.

My day job today is that of the COO of Zentech Inc. But I am at the stage in life where I can indulge in my passions. One of them has always been to package and sell a product called 'confidence'. To this effect, I teach students and help them through the complex college admissions process. I do this on weekends. The movement along the marginal utility curve for me with this adventure has been phenomenal and I cannot recount in words the immense satisfaction this gives me. My students stay in touch with me and I am blessed to have developed a deep relationship with all of them. They are my biggest teachers today.

Chapter 3

Contributing to the Motherland

Virendra Grover

Virendra Grover belongs to the early years when IIT was not a craze. There was no awareness about any particular branch or specific industry segment. Virendra did have a career goal—he wanted to pursue academics or R&D but had to adjust with the circumstances he was in.

Banking on his personal experience, Virendra is actively engaged on social media to provide career guidance and expertise on industry, technology trends, materials, energy and environment.

In recognition of Virendra's contribution to professional bodies, the Ghaziabad Management Association, an affiliate of All India Management Association, awarded him the Lifetime Achievement Award in 2021.

R. Nagarajan

R. Nagarajan is not your prototypical IITian. He never had much interest in science or engineering. He had IIT-dom thrust upon him in his 16th year. He refused to go for any JEE coaching, though, even way back in 1975, Brilliant Tutorials and a few others were in the business of coaching. He did go to evening JEE training classes at the college itself, if only to demonstrate his seriousness about the process. But inwardly, he was praying for failure. As fate would have it, he made it through and emerged from IIT Madras five years later as a certifiable chemical engineer.

Nagarajan used to average ten films and three novels per week during his five-year stay at Yale where he had joined a direct PhD programme. Despite the considerable distractions, he completed his PhD in about 4 years, at 25 years of age. In retrospect, what attracted him out of IIT-M to Yale was its starkly contrasting reputation as a liberal institution with strong programmes in arts and sciences. In his view, engineers are taught to act like robots. They ingest knowledge and output solutions. They are problem solvers, just like any well-designed piece of artificial intelligence. He believes real intelligence comes from developing an understanding of and appreciation for the world we live in. But now things have changed with more elective options at IIT.

Nagarajan joined IBM in San Jose, CA soon after a brief post-doctoral sojourn in Morgantown, WV, and rose through the ranks for 15 years like a good little IITian. In 2003, he was forced to relocate to Madras for personal reasons revolving around his ageing parents.

IIT-M beckoned him again. He joined the institute as a professor in the Department of Chemical Engineering in February 2004 and hasn't regretted it since. He served as the first-ever Dean at IIT Madras for International and Alumni Relations—encompassing fundraising—for nearly a decade. Recently he completed a three-year term as the head of the Department of Chemical Engineering. Now he is a free man again and looks forward to the resumption of hardcore academic pursuits, interspersed with leisure activities.

His reluctance to become an IIT student has been supplanted over the years by his pride in being associated with an elite institution of higher learning.

Rajendranath Kaura

The important takeaway for Rajendranath Kaura after studying at IIT was that five years of education prepared one for taking up any field. He started out with research activity at Bhabha Atomic

Research Centre at the Tata Institute of Fundamental Research. Then he shifted to marketing high-tech electronics and later set up a successful venture in a construction related activity. He believes that it is not important what business you are in, it is important how you conduct the business. Having realised that education has given him all that he has achieved, Rajendranath now supports the education of deserving and underprivileged students, under a scholarship programme called Vidya Daan. He believes you make a living out of what you get, but you make a life by what you give.

J. M. Thapar

J. M. Thapar is an alumni of IIT-D (M. Tech 1972-74). He is a self-made entrepreneur. He leveraged the strong technology foundation at IIT to set up and grow his electronics company across India. Currently, he is working to give back to society by conceptualising cost-optimised solutions for clean water and air using elementary concepts in science. Born in a middle-class family, he has not only made fortune for himself but has also contributed towards creating employment and helping the needy.

Anand Deshpande

Anand Deshpande left his cushy job in the USA at Hewlett Packard Laboratories in Palo Alto, California, where he worked as a Member of Technical Staff from May 1989 to October 1990. He is one of the few IIT Kharagpurians who came back to India to serve his motherland. In India, he started Persistent Systems. Today, Persistent Systems is a very successful Indian multinational and a publicly-traded global company. As a true technology visionary, Anand's strengths lie in identifying and investing in next-generation technologies and encouraging internal entrepreneurship to ensure that Persistent Systems stays at the forefront of technology innovation.

Anand is also a founding member of ISPIRT, India's first product think -tank, started with the vision of creating a vibrant entrepreneurial ecosystem in India. He is also a founder member of Inter Institutional Inclusive Innovations Centre (i4C). i4C is an independent, non-profit entity, which acts as a platform to pro-actively scout, showcase and handhold technology innovations, especially aimed at the base of the pyramid.

Anand's persistent hard work paid off when Forbes India included him in their list of billionaires in India in 2021. He was awarded the Distinguished Alumnus Award by IIT Kharagpur in 2012. He is currently the chairman of board of governors of IIT Patna and a part-time member of UID Authority of India.

Anand holds a B. Tech (hons) in computer science and engineering from IIT Kharagpur and an MS and a PhD in computer science from Indiana University, Bloomington, Indiana, USA.

Rajiv Vedi

Coming from a family of three generations of engineers, going to IIT-D was natural for Rajiv Vedi. The training at IIT-D helped him set up many factories for Times of India, for which the owners of the newspaper group (Jains) are forever grateful to him. He always stayed with the Jain family when travelling to Kolkata from Delhi and was taken always care of by them, like a family member. As he was an instrumentation expert, Rajiv was able to find a job in Australia quite comfortably, at the biggest Australian press, within a week of arriving in the country. He handled the job expertly. At a time when there weren't many Indian engineers in Australia, Rajiv contributed in building an image of excellence for Indian engineers among Australian employers. As a result, engineers migrating from the IITs in India are today picked up like 'hot cakes'.

Brijendra K. (BK) Syngal

Brijendra Syngal is popularly known as BK among his vast circle of friends worldwide. He is a pioneer in the Indian telecommunication sector, and has been referred to as the 'Father of Internet and Data Services in India'. He headed the stunningly ambitious effort to make India the first country in the developing world to launch its own satellite-based communication connectivity across oceans and the inaccessible hilly terrains of Leh, Ladakh, Spiti, Andaman and Nicobar. He was part of the team that prepared the blueprint for India's microwave networks. He has been at the cutting edge of technology throughout his life, living in the snake-infested jungles of Assam, the snowclad mountains of Kashmir, and the scorching heat of the Thar Desert. He was the first director in Indian National Satellite (INSAT) project in 1978. He is sought-after for his expert comments by the print and electronic media. He has addressed various forums on governance in public sector undertakings.

Brijendra joined VSNL in 1991 as its CMD, giving up a UN-job based out of London UK. He assisted Indian Space Research Organisation (ISRO) in the launch of its satellite in 1992.

Recently, Brijendra co-authored a book *Telecom Man* with another IIT Kharagpurian. It was printed, published and distributed worldwide by Amazon. He is one of the alumni who turned to reality Prime Minister Jawaharlal Nehru's dream during his address at the setting up of IIT Kharagpur, "Here in the place of that Hijli Detention Camp stands the fine monument of India, representing India's surges, India's future in the making."

Brijendra was instrumental in setting up the VSNL Chair at IIT Kharagpur and establishing scholarships for the needy in the name of his parents. The corpus stands at over Rs 1 crore.

Partha Sinha

Partha Sinha is currently the president of the Times Group where he is spearheading the response function. Partha started his career with Citi Bank NA, where he was the marketing manager for credit cards. Then he worked as the advertising, media and technology strategist across blue-chip companies such as Ogilvy, Zee, Publicis and BBH. Prior to joining the Times of India, he was the India Managing Director of McCann.

Partha is an alumnus of IIT Kharagpur and IIM Ahmedabad. He is also a columnist with business papers and teaches at IITs and IIMs.

Partha is an avid reader and a sports enthusiast and loves Indian classical music.

Stories from My Life

Prof Virendra Grover

1966-1971, B. Tech; Metallurgical Engineering IIT Kanpur

Born on January 7, 1947 in Ferozepur, I had the privilege of travelling to Lahore for a couple months, before moving back to India under highly tortuous circumstances (as narrated by my mother). My father, a commerce graduate, worked with Bank in Lahore, but I saw him selling charcoal and wood logs on Nasik Road in Maharashtra, when I was growing up.

My schooling commenced in Marathi followed by a year in Gangapur City in Rajasthan and then in Bareilly, UP, from third standard onwards. I had not heard of IIT or engineering till I passed 10+2 from Government Inter College. My career story and experiences can be a case study in SWOT analysis and I wish to share it for the benefit of the coming generations.

Education: 7 years at IIT Kanpur

The day I went to collect my 10+2 marks sheet in 1964, I learnt that some of my friends were going to IIT or Roorkee for engineering. It was too late for me to join these institutions, so I joined a two-year B. Sc course. Then I attempted to get into IIT the following year (1965). I was given the options of architecture, mining, agriculture and engineering at IIT Kharagpur, but my parents didn't agree to send me so far away.

A year later, I was not eligible for JEE due to the age limit, but the age stipulation was not present in 1966.

Thus, I landed in IIT Kanpur, opting for the metallurgical engineering stream. After the summer training at Tata Steel, I decided to pursue academics or R&D as a career choice.

I continued with an M. Tech at IIT Kanpur followed by being a research scholar at IIT Bombay.

Coming from a Hindi medium school, I had a tough time adjusting to the new environment in IIT, but this experience helped me learn to adjust and be a fluent speaker as well, as I participated in social activities.

There was overwhelming response to the campus visit of Swamy Chinmayanand in March 1967. Some of us from the first year decided to have weekly discussion meetings on Bhagavad Gita and formed the Vivekananda Samiti, which is now part of the Gymkhana. Besides spiritual sessions with stalwarts like Swami Ranganathananda of R. K. Mission, Viyogi Hari, an associate of Mahatma Gandhi, and many others, the Samiti launched a bi-weekly homeopathic dispensary in Nankari village, adjoining the campus. This was done through the voluntary services of Dr. Lal Chand Dhupar, the father of Professor B. L. Dhupar.

Opportunities and threats

Application for direct recruitment to R&D landed me in Alloy Steels Plant, Durgapur, a unit of the Steel Authority of India Ltd (SAIL). But I was not given an opportunity in research or plant operation. I was posted in shipping to dispatch steel products through trucks and railway wagons. This was purely an administrative job. I had to struggle for a shift to the training department. Then I moved to a private sector mini steel plant in northern India as a training officer.

Not satisfied with the work environment, I decided to leave the job in 1984. I did a couple of experiments in entrepreneurship for about two years. Then I joined the National Institute of Secondary Steel Technology, under the Ministry of Steel, Government of India, at Mandi Gobindgarh, a cluster of small steel mills in Punjab, as a senior training officer.

Here I published a bilingual (Hindi-English) quarterly *Bharatiya Dhatu Sandesh* for five years. The quarterly disseminated knowledge about metals, materials, energy and environment in simple language for the benefit of workers, supervisors and industry owners in order to raise awareness about the developments in technology. This was fully supported by the local industry and was distributed free during 1994-2000.

It was an opportunity to learn about the functioning of SMEs, besides mastering the practical aspects of energy conservation, while conducting field studies, lectures and workshops. Then I got an opportunity to work with a UNDP/GEF funded project of the Ministry of Steel, which aimed to reduce the carbon footprint of SMEs through improvements in energy efficiency. The objective was to promote advanced technologies that had many barriers; one of the barriers was the near total absence of qualified manpower (engineers and diploma holders) in the industry. Here I got an idea to float an NGO that would work to bring together the small industry and the engineering institutions, a concept called industry-academia collaboration. This was the Initiative to Support Promotion of Advanced Technologies, named ISPAT Bharti Foundation. This also aimed at providing career guidance and it is alive through a free monthly e-newsletter *Udyog Sanchetana*, since April 2014.

Career goal

It was a tough career journey from the day I left the public sector undertaking SAIL in 1981. That was the time when HR was a booming career. My desire to join a company as vice-president (HR) failed, because the employer wanted B Tech + MBA, not M. Tech, but thank god, I got an invitation from a consultancy company for the steel sector, named Korus Engineering Solutions Pvt Ltd to join as chief engineer (HRD and knowledge management). This accomplished my HR dream.

Korus represented 'chorus', a group singing activity, wherein individual weaknesses get covered in the collective voice of the team. It had the work environment of a family and didn't distinguish between the topmost and the junior-most staff. The job involved the use of my knowledge of metallurgy as well as my interest in training and HR management.

Lastly, an opportunity with Engineering Institution as professor and HoD (training), with the responsibilities of industry interaction, entrepreneurship and skill development, provided a close look at the current status of engineering education and its disconnect with the industry. Moreover, there is such a craze for IIT that over a million students aspire to study here every year, though the seats across the 23 IITs are not more than 11,000. This made me write a book titled *Dream IIT*, a career guide for engineering students. Another book in Hindi, *Ek Naya Virus Karodpati Engineer*, also had the same objective.

As an organiser and someone with an interest in social interaction, I initiated the founding of the Ghaziabad Management Association

(GMA) and established a chapter of the Indian Institute of Metals (IIM) in Mandi Gobindgarh. I was also charter secretary of Bharat Vikas Parishad, Ghaziabad and created TULSI in 2003 (Traffic-Transport Urban Life Systems Improvement). Operating in the area of household garbage management, TULSI initiated collection of clean kitchen waste from door to door (peels of fruits and vegetables) and the first roti (Indian bread) to be fed to cows. Started in August 2010, the free service has three rickshaws operating today, giving part-time employment to three people.

I have been an active member of professional societies and institutions like IIM, IEI, GMA, and Laghu Udyog Bharti, an all India body of SMEs. Interest in road safety made me write books in Hindi titled *Sadak Par* and *Aai Karen Traffic Control*, a book of rhymes for children.

I am active on social media and have 24K connections on LinkedIn and a page called 'Udyog Sanchetana', which means 'knowledge of industry'.

Website: http://ibf.org.in, www.EnMitra.com

Confessions of a Reluctant IITian

R. Nagarajan

1976-1981, B. Tech, IIT Madras

R. Nagarajan used to average ten films and three novels per week during his five-year stay at Yale where he had joined a direct PhD programme. Despite the considerable distractions, he completed his PhD in about 4 years, at 25 years of age. His reluctance to become an IIT student was supplanted over the years with his pride in being associated with an elite institution of higher learning.

I am not your prototypical IITian. I never had much interest in science or engineering. I had IIT-dom thrust upon me in my 16th year on this planet. I had made a deal with my parents that I would write the JEE, but if I failed to qualify, they would let me opt for my first and foremost love—English literature. Though I was educated in Mannargudi in the Tamil medium till eleventh standard, as it was known then, I got the first rank in English in the state in the SSLC examination, as it was known then. I did my P.U.C. as it was known then, (getting a tad repetitive, am I? You ain't seen nothing yet!) at Vivekananda College in Madras. My best and worst memory is standing up in an English class to read a poem review I had written, and having my classmates (especially the Vidya Mandir–Padma Seshadri coterie) yell, "He couldn't have written it himself!"

Talk about a bittersweet memory, that one was one sour-bitter lime and a sugary local sweet! That's when I knew I had some talent in English, even if I did pen a Wodehouse-rip-off for the college annual magazine.

I refused to go for JEE coaching, though, even way back in 1975, Brilliant Tutorials and a few others were in the business of coaching.

I did go to the evening JEE training classes at the college itself, if only to demonstrate my seriousness about the process. But inwardly, I was praying for failure. As fate would have it, I made it through and emerged from IIT Madras five years later as a certifiable chemical engineer.

But, upon graduation from the institute, I had an interesting choice to make. I received fellowships from two Ivy League schools—Brown and Yale. Those in the know urged me to choose Brown U, which had a much more solid reputation in engineering than Yale. I went through the promotional materials I had received from both the colleges very carefully and used a simple, yet powerful criterion to make my choice. I chose based on the number of film societies that each school had. As it turned out, in this category, Yale outnumbered Brown by a 5:1 margin. Voila! By September 1981, I was an Eli! I used to average 10 films and 3 novels a week during my 5-year stay at Yale. I was on a direct PhD programme, and, despite the considerable distractions, I completed my PhD in about 4 years, at 25 years of age.

I was married a year later, and my film-viewing and fiction-perusing habits dropped precipitously. I had a new distraction to distract me from my earlier distractions. Once the kids came, these pursuits dropped to nil, as I spent my time mainly (and vainly!) chasing the kids!

In retrospect, what attracted me, out of IITM, to Yale was its starkly contrasting reputation as a liberal institution with strong programmes in arts and sciences. In my view, engineers are taught to act like robots. We ingest knowledge and output solutions. We are problem solvers, just like any well-designed piece of artificial intelligence. But real intelligence comes from developing an understanding of and an appreciation for the world we live in.

Thinking back, I cannot recall a single course that dwelt on the sociological angle, across my five years at IIT-M. Even the German language we were taught was called 'Technical German'; the course content was carefully edited to ensure that all non-technical German was kept away from us. Our syllabus was claustrophobically engineering-based. Humanities were sneered at. Week-long workshops were welcomed. Even today, some of the older alumni yearn for those days of yore when they could saw away at a wooden piece for a full week. Great training for a budding robot, but, I'll vouch, a sure way to stifle the creativity of young and impressionable minds. Our previous director, Professor Ananth, made a conscious effort, amidst some opposition, to reduce the total number of credits that a UG must earn, as well as the total number of core courses a UG must take. In addition, UG students are now offered more elective options, including a greater variety of courses in humanities. The recently-introduced five-year integrated MA programme will, in my opinion, also be of great benefit to engineering students, who will now be exposed to more ideas and concepts that reflect the human condition. Students also now have more non-contact hours at their disposal. Hopefully, they will not waste these precious hours writing and solving equations.

My times were less enlightened. Sure, there were extra-curricular and co-curricular and anti-curricular activities outside the realm of engineering, but you indulged in these at your own risk. The faculty and administration looked down upon such 'infantile digressions'. Even today, there are many academics who would outlaw Saarang. I wonder if they realise that the erstwhile Mardi Gras was much more disgraceful in terms of the preponderance of sex, drugs and rock 'n' roll. But everyone loves Shaastra, because it is a techno-festival! When you blend technocracy with bureaucracy, you get a monster that feeds on keen minds and spits out dulled intellects, devoid of curiosity about the non-technical world around them. These are benighted souls, unaware that you cannot measure society with a slide rule, that you cannot compute culture with a calculator, that you cannot redress grievances by writing reports.

When I exited IIT, I was determined to rebel against the single-mindedly ferocious technological education. Hence, I immersed myself in all non-technical activities to the extent possible. I spent my measly grad school stipend ($450–$550 per month in those days) on books and videotapes to the extent that I subsisted on coffee for sustenance for the last two to three days of every month. I fell in love with baseball and American football from Day 1. The Mets and the Jets were my teams. Oh, and the Islanders in Ice Hockey! I hated the Boston teams, especially Red Sox, with all the passion of a typical New Haven resident. I was a patron of the Yale Repertory Theater from my first term at Yale. I attended the Philharmonic Orchestra performances in Woolsey Hall, as if I could really appreciate any of it. I played softball during the weekends, though I could never manage to keep the ball down. Long, lazy, fly-ball outs, that's me. I survived on pizza—two slices for lunch, two for dinner—since I hated to cook. I lived with American roommates, since very few Indians did so. Indian students roomed together, cooked together, and watched Hindi movies together. I guess I was really rebelling against my Indian-ness as much as I was against my hardcore engineering training.

I joined IBM in San Jose, CA soon after a brief post-doctoral sojourn in Morgantown, WV, and rose through the ranks for 15 years like a good little IITian. I discovered over time that I was pretty good at what I did, possibly the best in the world. Despite my misgivings about my chosen line of work, I had the professionalism to excel in it. But, during those years, I cut off all contact with IIT Madras as a collective entity, though I stayed in touch with a few friends. I did not attend Silicon Valley Chapter meetings, the 20th year reunion in Las Vegas, or any of the other IIT-flavoured gatherings. During my visits to Chennai, I steered clear of the IIT-M campus. I was not connected to any alumni Yahoo! groups. I did write a short story for *India Currents* on the theme of the push-and-pull forces acting on the average IITian (which won the second prize in the *Katha* competition that year), but apart from such occasional transgressions, I stayed aloof.

I classify the alumni who are passionately indulging in alumni associations into two categories: those displaying an 'aversion to adulthood' and those evincing a 'reversion to childhood'. I still believe this, even though I am now very much back in the IIT-M loop. In 2003, we were forced to relocate to Madras for personal reasons revolving around ageing parents. IIT-M beckoned me again. I joined the institute as a professor in the Department of Chemical Engineering in February 2004, and I haven't regretted it since. What is most heartening to me is that the rigidity of the curriculum has been replaced by a new-found passion to impart well-rounded learning.

I attended my first senate meeting (comprising the director, registrar, deans and professors) on the same day that I joined the faculty ranks. The first few issues to be discussed were the proposed reduction in core credits and overall credits and the increased emphasis on sciences and humanities. The timing couldn't have been more serendipitous. I'm a little ashamed to recall that my first reaction was to defend the status quo ("If five days of hacking at a metal piece was good enough for me, it is good enough for today's spoiled brats."). But wiser counsel prevailed. The institute was finally veering towards what I had sought desperately when I was a student—a more balanced educational experience, one that nurtured the left side of the brain as much as the right side. The female and male, yin and yang. Emotion versus logic. Intuition versus reasoning. When I talk to students, I encourage them to be open to non-scientific learning (not that they require much coaxing; most engineering students these days are ready to ditch their specialisations as soon as they graduate and seek greener pastures elsewhere). I also advise them to fly away from the coop that is

India and experience life elsewhere, even if it is for a short while. The 'guru-sishya' mode of education in India, where the teacher is held up as an object of worship, needs to be supplanted by a model wherein both are regarded as equals. A teacher is simply doing his or her job by teaching; there is no magic or mystery to it. It is a service profession, but how many teachers in India regard students as their 'customers', to whom they must provide a service? None, I dare say, particularly in the engineering arena where hierarchies are etched in concrete. The culture of dialogue is simply not present in technology schools; that is another reason why humanities faculty are needed to interact with and temper the training of engineering students. Dissent and discussion are the cornerstones of humanities education. Science and engineering are full of dogma.

My return to the IIT-M campus brought back some very good memories and a few not-so-edifying recollections. Like most alumni, my happiest remembrances revolve around the hostel, while the most painful ones are centred on the 'perios' (now renamed 'quizzes') that popped up twice a semester to everyone's discomfiture. It is a curious and instructive fact that most alumni would rather contribute to their individual hostel than to their parent department. The hostel environment was, of course, significantly more salubrious to one's overall development as an individual. The department

was a monolithic structure that intimidated more than it elevated. From HSB to MSB, it is but a short walk, but, during our student days, they seemed miles apart in their preoccupations. HSB was the window to the external world in all its fullness; it is not entirely a coincidence that the placement office is located in HSB. Even in the library, the stacks and stacks of technical volumes stood for never-ending boredom, whereas the few shelves with novels and light literature were like beacons of light in the prevailing gloom.

If my son or daughter ever gets into IIT, I hope they don't come out feeling like I did—that my entire education had consisted of reducing everything to mathematical formulae and solving them. For a long time after I graduated (heck, even now!), I had nightmares wherein I had to solve some equation or the other to escape certain death.

Education must necessarily be balanced to engage and nurture young minds. Engineering education, in particular, must involve a significant human component. English language skills must be honed. The student population entering IITs these days can hardly speak one full sentence in English; many lapse into their mother tongue halfway through a sentence because they are unable to complete the thought in English. English is the global language of communication. As national boundaries become insignificant, and a truly global village emerges, it is a fait accompli that English (and not flighty French, guttural German, sassy Spanish, cacophonous Chinese, or humdrum Hindi) must become the ipso facto linguistic standard. This is not chauvinism, just reality. It stands to reason then that spoken and written English language skills must be imparted to IIT students in steady doses (intravenously injected, if necessary) all through their stay on campus. By the time they leave, they must be able to make a technical presentation without getting hopelessly entangled in words; they should perhaps even be able to inject a little humour into the proceedings.

They must be like the Yalies, who are equally tuned into physics and metaphysics. IITs in general, and IIT Madras in particular, must become a great world university of the order of Yale, Harvard, Oxford and Cambridge. For that to happen, the institute must wean itself from a totalitarian engineering bent of mind and start expanding its horizons to include a greater assimilation of arts and sciences. I truly believe that IIT-M's vision and leadership is moving in that direction and I can only hope that future leaders continue this process of evolution. I look forward to the day when IIT Madras will not merely be in the top five of the world's engineering schools but in the top five of educational institutions, period.

I served as the first-ever dean at IIT Madras for international and alumni relations—encompassing fundraising—for nearly a decade, and, recently, I completed a three-year term as the head of the Department of Chemical Engineering. Now I am a free man again and I look forward to resumption of hardcore academic pursuits, interspersed with leisure activities. My reluctance to become an IIT student has been supplanted over the years by my pride in being associated with such an elite institution. Ah, the follies of youth!

Make a Living Out of What You Get But Make a Life by What You Give

Rajendranath Kaura

1961-1966, B. Tech, Electrical Engineering, Shivalik House, IIT Delhi

> *After studying at IIT, Rajendranath Kaur learnt that five years of education prepared one for taking up any field. He started with research activity at Bhabha Atomic Research Centre at Tata Institute of Fundamental Research, before shifting to marketing high-tech electronics. Then he set up a successful venture in construction related activity. He believes you make a living out of what you get but make a life by what you give.*

Formative years

I was born in 1943 in the border town of Ferozepur. My family did not have to go through the trauma of being uprooted during Partition but they witnessed the horrors of merciless killings that occurred during that time. Train loads of people killed across the border would arrive along with a few fortunate ones who reached alive.

One more significant event was a massive flood in 1947 when our bungalow was under nearly one foot of water and all children were carried on the backs of elders to our neighbour's house, which was fortunately constructed on a plinth of over two feet. We were all awake the whole night, measuring, with sticks, the levels the water had reached. Fortunately, it receded after a few days.

My parents moved to Delhi seeing greater opportunities there, and I finished my schooling in Salwan School. I was a shy and studious boy and was not very well-known in the school. When I completed

11th standard as a topper in the school, everyone referred me as the younger brother of my brother, who was very well-known, being a sports person and a popular figure.

IIT entrance

When we joined IIT Delhi in its first batch, it was called the College of Engineering and Technology, with the participation of faculty from the UK. It was a common sight to see our maths professor urging all of us to hurry up to reach our classes on time. Two years later, the institute was renamed 'IIT Delhi'.

It started with five small buildings, one for each branch of engineering and two hostels, Shivalik and Vindhyachal. Roads were mud roads and, in the rains, it was quite an experience reaching the classrooms from the hostel, navigating through the water pools and slush.

The main road was nearly 3 km from the hostel, with very few lamp posts. It was a very scary experience to walk alone from the main road to the hostel on a Sunday, late in the evening, especially after reading *Horror of Dracula* the previous week.

We were fortunate that there was no ragging by the seniors since we were the first batch.

Principle R. N. Dogra and Mrs Dogra took personal interest in ensuring that our stay in the hostels was comfortable. They even hosted many dinners at their sprawling campus bungalow.

Being in the same hostel for five years helped us develop a special bond, which is still a strong force. The college's golden anniversary was very well attended in 2016.

Many of us had not met each other for 50 years. But it took us only a few minutes for us to start calling each other by the college nicknames—Shorty, Cylinder and so on.

Prince Charles' visit to our college in 1964 was a memorable occasion. All of us were introduced to him. One of our batchmates, who was part of the hockey team, introduced himself as, "I am Hockey, sir" to which Prince Charles promptly replied, "I am Polo, sir."

Professional experience

I was very keen to join a research organisation and was fortunate to be selected for training at Bhabha Atomic Research Centre (BARC). After one year of training, we had the option to join Tata Institute of Fundamental Research (TIFR) or BARC.

I opted to join the computer group of TIFR and was soon heading the hardware group engaged in the development of an air defence project. It exposed me to the latest in computers and electronics. TIFR had a huge computer from Control Data Corporation housed in a very big hall. It would today be the equivalent of a laptop computer. It was a common sight to see engineers rushing around, with a bunch of punched data cards.

After working for seven years in TIFR, my enthusiasm for active research started dipping and I began to look for an opening in electronics marketing. I was fortunate to come in contact with a start-up engaged in marketing, in India, semiconductor products of frontline companies like Fairchild Semiconductor.

It was a great experience to travel extensively across the USA and know about the latest in semiconductors, components and manufacturing equipment. In those days, we used to travel with limited foreign exchange and it was quite an experience to save some dollars to buy goodies for the home and the children at home.

Since Bangalore was the main centre for top public centre companies like ITI, BEL, LRDE and ADE, I shifted my base to Bangalore in 1977 and I am still in Bangalore.

In a totally unexpected move, in 1992, I got into a business connected with construction and waterproofing of buildings and it became a successful venture.

What you can see from the flow of my profession—from active research to electronics marketing to construction related business—is that ideas change over a period of time; preconceived ideas like 'doing only research' can see a dramatic turn. One has to flow with the current and not resist too much. Our education teaches us to absorb learnings from different fields and succeed.

It is not important what business one is doing, but what is important is how a business is run. Values like customer satisfaction, ethics and employee retention are important.

Rotary experience

It was in 1987 that I was introduced to Rotary by a good friend. I found in this an opportunity to give back to society what I had received in abundance. While there are many avenues of service, I found my passion in providing help to the needy and underprivileged. In my opinion, the biggest help we can provide is financial help to the unfortunate sections of society. There are many students who are capable but are not able to pursue higher education because of financial constraints. That is where our scholarship project 'Vidya Daan' steps in. Currently, over 500 students are being supported in this programme.

We make a living by what we get but we make a life by what we give. Our mission is to reach that critical mass when our graduated students are able to support all our new students and the project becomes self-sustaining.

General experience

Always keep an open mind and never feel that you have reached a stage in life wherein no more learning is possible. Always engage yourself by reading books of diverse subjects.

Currently, I am actively engaged in attending astrology classes at the age of 78 years. It has opened an entirely different dimension in my thinking.

Nothing happens by chance. It is your actions that determine the future. Circumstances are pre-determined but your free will decides the outcome. Life is not fatalistic but is probabilistic. Hope you find some value in my sharing of my life experiences.

Giving Back to Society and Conceptualising Cost-Optimised Solutions

J. M. Thapar

1972-74, M. Tech, Electronics, IIT Delhi

> *J. M. Thapar is a self-made entrepreneur. He leveraged the strong technology foundation at IIT to set up and grow his electronics company across India. Currently, he is working to give back to society by conceptualising cost-optimised solutions for clean water and air using elementary concepts in science. Born in a middle-class family, he has not only made fortune for his own self but has also contributed towards creating employment and helping the needy.*

I am the youngest in a family of three sisters and two brothers. I was always a good student. My father J. L. Thapar was the principal of DAV School and one of the finest physics teachers of his time. He was the first to deliver physics lectures in educational TV programmes in India. My mother, Tara Vati, is well educated too. Being born to educated parents, the value of good education was always known to me and was prioritised in the family.

I passed higher secondary from DAV School in 1967. Then I cleared the IIT entrance exam and joined IIT Delhi. However, due to my inherited interest in physics, I left IIT-D to join B. Sc. Physics (honours) at Delhi University. Then I completed M.Sc. Physics. My ambition was to work for the improvement of the lives of blind people; so I decided to do a PhD at All India Institute of Medical Sciences, Delhi, in its ophthalmology department. But to fulfil the wish of my parents, I changed my mind and joined M. Tech at IIT Delhi and specialised in electronics. I secured the second position here.

Education at IIT-D

The education methodology at IIT helps you to develop strong logical reasoning. Getting an education from the premier technical institute had a profound impact on my reasoning and thinking. Probably that was the reason why, like many other IITians, I could start my own company at a young age.

My transition from being a hardcore R&D person to being an entrepreneur is an interesting one. But, before I get into that, let me tell you the story of getting my first job, which is equally interesting. There was a campus interview, but I preferred to go home. Even after a long wait at the bus stand, I did not get the bus to go home. It was time for the interview; so I decided to attend the interview. Luck favoured me and I got the job. Due to my IIT-D background, I got more salary than I demanded. Thereafter, getting a better job in companies of my choice was very easy.

In 1974, I started my career as an R&D engineer with Televista Electronics, a renowned TV manufacturing company then. Later I worked with a few other companies like Weston, DCM

Data Products and Uptron. I spent 10 quality years in the electronics industry in developing and designing hardcore electronics.

As luck would have it, at DCM, I had a difference of opinion with my manager, and I was forced to leave my job. Thereafter, I went through a tough financial situation. I started a small business of calculator assembly for Weston Electronics, my old employer, in April 1980. During this period, I lost my father, who was my inspiration and guide. In June 1980, I got a managerial position at Uptron in its computer division. Here I got a chance to work with renowned R&D engineer Mr Gaffar and learned a lot from him.

My wife Lalita, who is also an engineer, had a desire to start a business. She started her company in 1982. She forayed into manufacturing of office furniture. I joined the company in 1984. Soon we were approached with a requirement for a UPS from the person who had been responsible for my exit from DCM. He was aware of my understanding of electronics. He wanted me to make a UPS to be displayed alongside his company's newly launched computer. I took on the task and developed a UPS in a few days. At the exhibition, our UPS was displayed along with the new computer. During this exhibition, a lot of computer manufacturers and users came to know about us. In those times, there were hardly any companies manufacturing UPS in India. Due to my strong R&D experience and attitude of solving problems, instilled at IIT, I decided to take up the challenge and designed a range of UPS.

As they say, one of the most critical factors of success is timing. The very same year, Rajiv Gandhi became the prime minister of India. Due to his vision of modernisation, computerisation became very popular in the country and so did our product.

Our company was called Shah Sahib Electronics, the name given to us by our Guruji Shah Sahibji. While I managed the technical and manufacturing activities of the company, my wife Lalita led the commercial activities. The company took off to a flying start. In the early days, we managed to secure more than 50% market share in banks, life insurance corporations, general insurance, and a lot of private industries and offices throughout India.

We purchased our own offices in almost all cities where banks had their head offices. Not only did our flourishing business help me make a fortune for myself and my family, but it also allowed me to serve society. I could sponsor the education of a few needy students and extend financial support to our staff in their hour of need.

I could also finance the setting up of a physics laboratory at DAV School, in loving memory of my father, J. L. Thapar, who always went the extra mile to help students to be successful in their life.

Spiritual journey

After seeing roaring success in business for 14 years, there was no looking back, until an accident put the brakes on our journey. My wife and I met with a road accident in 1998. Due to head injuries, I could not take care of the business for two years. In this period, many competitors came up. Though we forayed into new products, our enthusiasm and success were never the same again.

This was partly due to the fact that I had repurposed my life. While recovering from a severe depression post my accident, I was helped by Satguru Lakshmi Bhagwan. She was the reason we developed a keen interest in spiritualism. With the quest for more, we met several saints to understand the real purpose of life. Meanwhile, my daughter and son were well settled in life; so we decided to close our business in 2015 to spend more time in spiritual activities.

Work for social welfare

After closing our business, we decided to serve society in our own way. Lalita started preaching the concept of life and God, as she had learnt from Satguru Lakshmi Bhagwan, and helping people solve their family problems. I too learned the new meaning of life, which is above the materialistic world. I started helping the needy and devoted a lot of time to help people who were depressed and deprived of happiness in life. To be of some use to other people has become our motive in life.

We adopted four children to help them complete their school education. We also help the needy people financially for medical treatment. We also partially finance the wedding of many women.

I decided to give back to society by developing concepts for clean water and air. My education at IIT and the university about basic science could be put to effective use. I am now working on conceptualising a few sustainable projects like flood water harvesting, air pollution management, and water production through desalination of seawater using solar energy.

I look forward to a breakthrough in developing pure, low-cost, easily accessible solutions for clean water and air for the masses. This would be my true redemption and reparation to the education received at a premiere institute, nurturing the best of engineers, with the highest quality of education to date.

Brief about the projects

- Pollution reduction in air using water as a filter: In my lab experiments, I have been able to improve the air quality (both PM 10 and PM 2.5) from 999 to less than 50. The results have been acknowledged by a professor at IIT-D and forwarded to the pollution control department of Delhi. The paper was published in a leading technology magazine.
- Flood water harvesting during floods: The solution is designed not only to safeguard people and property from floods each year but also to recharge the fast-depleting groundwater. The concept was appreciated by a professor at IIT Delhi and was also published in NRDC Journal.
- Low-cost clean water generation at a large scale through desalination of seawater using solar energy: The unique concept is well acknowledged and appreciated by a scientist at the Department of Earth Sciences in India. The department is evaluating the feasibility of implementing the concept. The technique estimated production of 5000 litres/hour for 1 paisa/litre. Moreover, the project would cost a fraction of the current set-up costs in India (for similar capacity) and a far lower OPEX.

Road to Success and Lifelong Friends

Dr. Anand Deshpande

1979-84, B. Tech (Hons) - Computer Science Engineering, Patel Hall, IIT Kharagpur

At IIT Kharagpur, Dr. Anand Deshpande learnt how to network with fellow students from different backgrounds and different parts of the country, learning how to accept different points of view. The experience provided during the late-night 'Bhat sessions', where one learnt to argue on all kinds of topics, helped him build confidence in his ability to have logical conversations on diverse topics. At IIT, Anand and his classmates 'wasted' a lot of time together. But looking back, the people he 'wasted' most time with continue to be his best friends. All of Anand's classmates have done well in their careers and become senior executives in their companies. Clearly, the wasted time was not such a waste after all!

My five years in IIT Kharagpur were very influential and set me upon a solid foundation for the rest of my life. I first landed at Patel Hall, IIT Kharagpur, on July 12, 1979, as a young 17-year-old. It was a proud moment for me as after a year-and-a-half of hard work, preparing for JEE. And I was finally there. Everyone who joins IIT remembers their All India Rank for life. My rank was 1285 and I got into aeronautical engineering. With aero and Anand, my roll number was 1 for all the five years at IIT.

As roll number 1, I would be the first one for all the viva and orals. Perhaps my paper was also the first one to be graded. Being the first for orals had mixed benefits. The professors would not have had an opportunity to calibrate the students and they would often start with the most challenging questions first. The kind of questions you could get asked was also a kind of wild guess. I figured that every viva had a time allocated to it, and the best strategy for me was to consume enough time by providing detailed answers for the warm-up questions. This strategy of analysing the best use of time for a meeting has helped me plan my sales calls. If you can get customers to share their own stories, they will most likely remember the meeting.

Very early on at IIT, I learnt the power of positive thinking and inculcated a can-do attitude in myself. I was a regular student, and grades happened through the discipline of completing assignments on time and by pushing hard for a week before the exams. This left me with enough time to pursue other activities. We all had many things to do, and we learned how to prioritise time for the best results.

While I started out in aeronautical engineering, I was fortunate enough to move to computer science and engineering in my third year. IIT Kharagpur had decided that it would be the first IIT to graduate a batch of computer science and engineering students. The two batches that graduated in 1982 and 1983 and our batch in 1984 were admitted directly into the third year. Our batch of computer science and engineering was intense, but we were a very close-knit unit.

One incident that comes to mind happened during our fourth year. It was just a week before the pooja holidays, and there was an encephalitis scare on campus. A few students got sick, and some others in the area even died. With just one week of classes left before the scheduled holiday, it was very tempting to skip the classes for a week for an extended vacation. As a result, many students left campus, and some were planning mass cuts. Our class decided that we should ask for permission, and I was chosen to plead the case.

Along with a couple of classmates, I met Professor Pal Chaudhuri and asked him if we could take a week off. He was quite surprised that someone was actually asking permission for the entire class to bunk a week of classes. He thought for a moment and then said yes. I learnt something from this incident. Even in the most awkward situations, it doesn't hurt to ask.

While most of us left for home, some local students stayed back to practise for the inter-IIT games. Professor Pal Chaudhuri saw my classmates, Amarnath and Parikshit, on campus and asked them to attend class. We had perfect class unity, and Amarnath and Parikshit flatly refused. They told Prof Pal Chaudhuri that it was our joint decision to leave, and since many classmates had gone to their hometowns and could not be back in time, all of us would miss class, and we would face the consequences together. I am sure professor was very angry at that time, but he admired us for our unity in the long run.

Patel Hall was always the most enthusiastic and energetic hostel on campus. We always had the first few rows in Netaji Auditorium blocked for us for the Friday night movies, and there was no shortage of excitement all through the night, especially during power failure. My wing mates, Suresh, KLV, Himanshu, Ashutosh, Kartar, Rampal and Vinay, were always active in sports and hall politics. We always adopted a few juniors, and they would 'hang out' in our wing. Vinay and I had a great time organising the 'Perpendicular Patel Olympics'. We included sports such as Gilli-Danda, Marbles, Cycle Polo, 29 and Treasure Hunt. These events were a great hit.

I was part of the IIT swimming and water polo teams. During my final year, we won the inter-hall water polo championship.

Kharagpur was an oasis in the middle of nowhere. I was fortunate to have had the opportunity to obtain excellent education, practically for free. The friends I made here have stayed with me all through these years.

At IIT Kharagpur, I learnt how to network with fellow students from different backgrounds and different parts of the country. We learned how to accept different points of view. The experience provided during the late-night 'Bhat sessions', where one learnt to argue on all kinds of topics, helped me build confidence in my ability to have logical conversations on diverse topics. We wasted a lot of time together. But, as I look back, the people I wasted most time with continue to be my best friends. All my classmates have done well in their careers and have become senior executives in their companies. Clearly, the wasted time was not such a waste after all!

During the early 80s, going to the US for higher education was a big craze. Many students would apply for US admissions, and most of them would get scholarships. The entire process was expensive and tedious. It was the early 80s, and we had to send pre-app aerogrammes to get application forms. Every application required a fee of $25 to $50, which was a significant sum of money in those days. We had limited knowledge of the process, and much of the intelligence was obtained from what our seniors handed down to us. The application process was secretive, and students would not share the places they were applying to. We decided to change this. I conducted a meeting for all our classmates and I convinced them that it was in everyone's interest to be transparent through this process. I built a large table to ensure that a professor wrote a recommendation letter for only one student per university. Spreadsheets did not exist then, but we built a nice three-dimensional pivot to ensure that the admissions office could not directly compare two recommendation letters.

As part of our application packet, it was customary to include a short overview of our courses. We had those cyclostyled sheets, which were hard to read. A dozen pages in airmail made the package heavy and expensive. In my fourth year, I had been the secretary of the Computer Society, and I had spent hours with the printing press in Chhota Tengra, printing our annual magazine *The Interface*. It took a little effort to convince all our classmates to shell some money, and we all got the entire syllabus printed on one large sheet, which folded out attractively. I ended up doing my MS and PhD in computer science at Indiana University, Bloomington, Indiana, USA in 1986 and 1989. In 2007, I received a Career Achievement Award from Indiana University.

As part of the Computer Society of the department at IIT, a friend and I took responsibility for printing the annual souvenir *The Interface*. We needed advertisements for the magazine, and that gave me my first experience of being a salesman. While we got rejects from many companies, I have fond memories of visiting Arjun Malhotra, Co-founder of HCL, at his Nehru Place office. Arjun is an IIT Kharagpur alumnus. After chatting with me for a few minutes, he agreed to sponsor the back cover page. I found my meeting with Arjun very inspiring, and I have stayed in touch with him ever since.

One more interesting story is related to my B. Tech thesis. Pradeep Sinha and I were partners, and we were responsible for doing a project on implementation for relational databases. 'Query By Example' was an innovative IBM product, and our professor encouraged us to take a look at that. I decided to send a handwritten aerogramme to Dr. Moshe Zloof, the architect of Query By Example and the manager of the database group at IBM Yorktown Heights. I was delighted when I got a friendly letter on an IBM letterhead from Dr. Zloof. He sent me a few reprints of his papers and encouraged me to work in this area.

I stayed on with databases through my PhD and continued to work in this area till date. I had the opportunity to meet Dr. Zloof when he joined Hewlett Packard Laboratories, where I was an employee in 1989-90. I mentioned to Dr. Moshe that I had written to him when I was a student and thanked him for his reply. I was even more elated when Dr. Moshe said that he remembered the correspondence as he found it odd to have received a handwritten aerogramme from a student in India. I have stayed in touch with Dr. Moshe, and I count on him to be my mentor and advisor whenever I need advice.

At IIT, I learnt how to take a chance, convince and sell. These skills have helped me through my journey at Persistent. Another skill that I learnt was how to manage money. I was an NTS scholar during my

IIT tenure, but the scholarship would never come on time. We had to budget our cash needs and write letters to our parents to get a cheque, which took several weeks to cash. What we would celebrate on would depend on cash in the bank account—Waldorf, Chhedis or the canteen on B-First.

Sometimes strange coincidences happened. During our final year, job placement was a big deal. Though I was planning to go abroad for higher studies, getting a job offer was important. TCS was one of the first companies to come to campus. The company had an elaborate form, which we were asked us to fill in as part of the interview process. One of the questions on the form was "What do you see yourself as in ten years?" I remember writing that I saw myself as the general manager in the company. The interviewer was perhaps not expecting such an arrogant answer and asked me to explain. During the interview, I defended my position with confidence and said, "If I don't get to do this at TCS, I would undoubtedly do it elsewhere." I did not get an offer from TCS.

In 1992, after I had started Persistent Systems, I visited the Tata Research Centre (TRDDC) in Pune. By then, I was the CEO of my small company. While I was in the lobby, I ran into the person who had been on my interview panel. He remembered me and asked me what I was doing. He was pretty impressed when I shared my CEO business card with him.

I am the Founder, Chairman and Managing Director of Persistent Systems Limited. It was established in 1990 and listed in 2010. The company employs over 14,500 employees in 18 countries. The FY21 revenues exceeded $566 million and has a market cap of $3.8 billion. I am also the founder of deAsra Foundation, a personal philanthropy organisation, driving success for the self-employed. More than 120,000 entrepreneurs have been supported so far and counting!

Engineering Family Leaves a Mark in Australia

Rajiv Vedi

1972-1977, Control and Instrumentation, Vindhyachal Hall, IITDelhi

> *Coming from a family of three generations of engineers, going to IIT Delhi was natural for Rajiv Vedi. An instrumentation expert, Rajiv found it quite comfortable to find a job in Australia, with the biggest Australian press within a week of arrival in the country. He handled the job expertly. At a time when there weren't many Indian engineers in Australia, Vedi contributed in building the image of excellence of Indian engineers among Australian employers. As a result, engineers migrating from IITs in India are today picked up like hot cakes.*

Born and brought up in a family of engineers for three generations, engineering and technology was naturally fed to us from early childhood. This was the strong driving force for me to pursue engineering and join IIT Delhi.

Late-night hard work during exam time and walks up to JNU campus for midnight tea during the exams are wonderful memories. Finally, the time came, after submitting the final M. Tech thesis. There were no more classes to attend; it was time to say goodbye to the institute and the department. I had mixed feelings of happiness and sadness. I was happy for there no more classes, assignments and tutorials, but I was sad that I would miss my friends, the department and the IIT environment. We batchmates were in a dream world, still in Vindhyachal Hostel counting our last days together. A few had already taken up jobs, through campus selection, with multinationals.

Someone suggested sitting for the BHEL engineer trainee entrance exam. So I decided to take up the test. And soon came the day when we were all set and ready for the final exam of our lives. It was a surprise to me as it was a cake walk. Most questions in the paper were similar, if not the same, to the question in our regular monthly tutorial tests. The good thing about the BHEL exam was that only 'pass' or 'fail' was announced; there was no mark or rank during those days. I see this now as very positive thing as it eliminates any comparative or superiority feelings among colleagues.

Soon came the first day of job at BHEL. After one week of orientation, everyone was called in by the HR head and the CMD for final allocation of the department to continue the 'dream team'. That was the first time I learnt the value of being an IIT-D alumni. I was told me that because I was from IIT-D and I also had an M. Tech, they were offering me a position in the design and engineering division. This was considered a top-ranking placement, which was in demand by everyone. I was not sure why it was so, may be because the job was positioned in Delhi.

After working on the engineering design of thermal power stations for just a month, I took a transfer to the projects division to gain a hands-on field experience. I was again assigned the area of my choice; since I had a background of control and instrumentation, I was made responsible for the main central control room at the huge thermal power station. The entire control room, the heart and hub of the thermal power station, became my area of expertise and paid me a long way in life.

My next breakthrough was at the Times of India, during its modernisation phase as the group moved to digital printing, eliminating many interim production stages of conventional printing. During that time, I got involved in setting up few new printing houses around the country, for around 10 years, before migrating to Australia.

The unique training at IIT-D and the rich experience I gained at Times of India kept rewarding me throughout my time in Australia.

I thank my choice of IIT-D almost half a century ago.

The Tomorrow I Knew Little About

B. Syngal

*1956-1961, B. Tech (Hons); Electronics and
Telecommunications, IIT Kharagpur*

Brijendra Syngal is a pioneer in the Indian telecommunication sector and has been referred to as the 'Father of Internet and Data Services in India'. He headed the stunningly ambitious effort to make India the first country in the developing world to launch its own satellite-based communication connectivity across oceans and the inaccessible hilly terrains of Leh, Ladakh, Spiti, Andaman and Nicobar. He was also the first director in INSAT (Indian National Satellite project) in 1978. He joined VSNL in 1991 as its CMD, giving up a UN job based out of London, UK. He assisted the Indian Space Research Organisation in the launch of its satellite in 1992.

Let me begin by saying that I am who I am because of these three institutions: my parents, my teachers and my alma mater.

Let me first begin with the latter—the institute. Well, it gave me the most important foundation of life, i.e., knowledge. Today, we all say knowledge is power, the oft repeated mantra of the 21st century. But if we explore and dig deep into our scriptures, we will find that our sages and Vedas had said so, thousands of years ago, "*Yasya budhi tasya balam.*" This translates to this, "Those possessing capability and knowledge possess strength."

Knowledge is the basis of that foundation that makes you stand up and face any challenge in the world; though, in the present day, one must be armed with information, foresight and wisdom to use the knowledge to achieve what one wishes to in life.

The journey to Kharagpur

Having said that, let me step back about 60 years ago to the beginning of my journey with IIT Kharagpur, which then was the one and only one IIT.

It was during the summer of 1955 that inspiration came from a cousin who was interviewed and was admitted to IIT Kharagpur—the newest of the prestigious institutes in the country. He was one of 20,000 people who competed from all over India for a place among 250 seats. He ended up being a gold medallist here in 1959.

The very name 'Kharagpur' made people stand up. It lit a fire in the belly. There was no designer coaching classes. It was that fire and the encouragement by parents that led me to prepare for the IIT entrance exams two years later. This cousin was the icon for all of us in the clan.

It was in June 1957, the year the first satellite Sputnik was launched by the then Soviet Union, that the ultimate happened. Imagine my delight and surprise when the postman brought that registered letter from IIT Kharagpur's assistant registrar's office for an interview, before being accepted for admission. Finally, I landed at Kharagpur escorted by my father to join the electrical engineering department.

However, I chose electronics and telecommunications after two years. It was that urge to go beyond the horizon to the nether world of the UNKNOWN. There was an uproar that I would be famished and die in harness, but there was that desire to connect people. As children, we saw that telephones were a luxury and getting connected meant a wait of at least 12 hours for a long-distance call.

Gentlemen, here I am. That was a risky but courageous decision. As Richard Nixon once said, "If you do not take risks, you do not make mistakes, if you do not make mistakes, you do not learn, and if you do not learn, you do not win wars." Well, I took that risk.

Who would have reckoned then that electronics and telecom would become the fourth dimension of transportation after land, sea and air, carrying trillions of bytes of information, making people talk of the digital divide or think at the speed of light!

People want to connect, machines want to connect, and businesses want to connect. It is connectivity that is required today and that is what telecom is all about. Connectivity. Well, today it looks so simple. No wonder that there is this a mad scramble and fight to get into these disciplines of cyberspace when they went a begging in the fifties.

IIT taught me that competition is the name of the game and you have to be better than the best. IIT also honed the skills to see things through, envision, plan and stay steps ahead and execute. I think I learnt more outside the classroom than inside it.

IIT Kharagpur was somewhat like a gurukul. I loved my IIT years. You were dropped into the deep end to fend for yourself. You were far removed from the protection and luxuries of your home, away from the trappings of city life and the tutelage of your parents, except for the monthly budget of rupees 125. In some cases, it could be 30 percent of the parents' earnings. That is where the sacrifices of the parents came in. A postman was the link to your parents unlike SMS, cellphones and e-mails of today. IIT was the true melting pot of India and the world. We came from all over the country, and a few came from outside India. The academy was international too. It taught me independence and cross-cultural understanding. It was my first real opportunity to understand and respect the motivations, emotions and sentiments behind so many different individuals. IIT helped me build and nurture long-term relationships and friendships.

IIT taught me how to budget (rupees 125) and how to live within the budget. It taught me the meaning of responsibility. No one ever forced you to study, but everyone did. It taught me equality and the ability to stand on my own two feet.

Days at IIT

Life at Kharagpur was tough. The water would run out mid-shower. And you stood there with soap all over the body, screaming for help, for someone to come down with a bucket filled with water collected from the stored water.

In those days, there was no slogan shouting. Director Sengupta's no non-sense approach, decisiveness and aura are qualities that I admire to this day. His conviction, authority and unwavering 'no option, no-nonsense' approach were all lessons well learnt.

Beyond IIT

I left IIT Kharagpur in 1962, with both a B. Tech (honours) and an M. Tech. It was time to face the world and the challenges ahead. A job at the electronics firm Philips beckoned. Although the money was great in the private sector, the spectrum was limited, and I soon got bored.

The jobs in the private sector did not offer a wide range of opportunities in any field, save TVs, audio amplifiers and radio sets.

I applied to the government's technical service and got through. Most of my cousins and bright friends had done so. I was appointed in a department where the corruption was far too much for me to handle; it was not my cup of tea. My stay here was short but not sweet. So, I sat for exams again the next year and this time I got into Telegraph Engineering Service, the most coveted department then in telecom. I took a salary cut at rupees 420 a month. But I saw my dream of connecting people become a reality, in real time. Most of my fellow batchmates chose cushy jobs, like being a sub-divisional officer, but I opted for project execution, i.e., in the business of installing equipment.

Life was hard because I was setting up the first of the microwave networks in the difficult jungle-and-mountain terrains of Assam and

Kashmir and coaxial cable systems in the deserts of Rajasthan. But it was a totally satisfying work. In those years, I worked as a mason, I worked as a carpenter. I have done tamping and concreting and grouting, I have installed and even overhauled engine alternators. It was exciting work, living in the jungles of Assam, in the snow of Srinagar, in the heat and dust of Rajasthan, at times in the Swiss cottage tents, away from any civilisation, in the company of leopards, bears, snakes and leeches, and under moonlit starry nights, with the accompaniment of the sounds of the water flowing over the pebbles.

I could do all that because of the tempering of going through the cold and hot cycles to produce good steel frame provided by none other than where I stand today—in front of all of you. If you can withstood the IIT Hermitage, you are fit for anywhere, any situation, any challenge in the world.

In 1972, I was shifted to the headquarters in Delhi, as part of the team that prepared the blueprint for India's microwave networks. After some good hard work, I got a diplomatic assignment at the Embassy of India in Budapest, Hungary. Those years were yet another learning experience of living in a closed environment. Hungary was then part of the Eastern European Block under the Soviet Union. We decided to live outside the diplomatic fortress. That offered us an opportunity to learn the language and understand the people and their culture. It was fun to be able to interact with a society where no other language was spoken.

In 1978, back home after a three-year stint at Budapest as technical attaché at the Indian embassy, I told the government that I wanted to lead India's nascent satellite programme. My colleagues told me that I was mad to be venturing into areas where angels feared to tread. But I wanted a challenge and this was a challenge. As the first director of the INSAT (Indian National Satellite) project, I headed a stunningly ambitious effort that would make India the first country in the developing world to launch its own communication satellite-based connectivity across oceans and the inaccessible hilly terrains of Leh, Ladakh, Spiti, Andaman and Nicobar. It was a challenge in terms of time, budget and technology, but the INSAT project was completed within the defined parameters. Its importance could be underlined by the fact that it was monitored by the then Prime Minister, Mrs Gandhi. The joy of doing, delivering and honouring the commitments made when accepting the assignment was very special indeed.

Again in 1982, in recognition of the good work, I was sent as India's nominee on secondment to Inmarsat in London. It was another a dive into the deep end to work on cutting-edge technology. Despite being there for nine fruitful years, there was something missing in my work in a foreign environment. The money was there to be had, but the fizz had gone. You are discriminated against, however subtly; hence you never belong to that part. The family took a very painful and hard decision, and we came back. Had it not been for the support of the family, perhaps I would not have. That is why I say that, after parents and teachers, you have peers/friends, superiors and family, without whose support one is nothing.

VSNL

It was in 1991 that I came across an article in the *Economist*—'The Caged Tiger Raring to Go'. I thought to myself, *Why should not I be the part of that revolution?* It was so compelling to come back and accept the challenge of improving connectivity for anything to connect to anything, at all times, at 100%. That very tough challenge made me decide that I must go back, giving up a cushy well-paid tax-free job and fancy cars. My golden era began when I was offered a simple deal: *If you want to make money, don't come back to India. If you want a challenge, come to VSNL. Unleash the tiger.*

The West had given me to understand a few very important facets of life—equality, economic well-being, and quality of life. I went to a dreary telephone monopoly and left behind a customer-focused multimedia market leader.

We introduced internet and digital connectivity in India in 1995 and presided over its explosive growth. Most historical accounts of the Indian software industry boom would remain incomplete if they did not highlight the contributions of VSNL.

VSNL was one of the top ten companies in market capitalisation and other parameters at BSE and NSE, among public and private sector companies. It was ranked in the first 30 at LSE.

I am proud to have been part of the breed of engineers who built India's giant public sector corporations—men who resisted the much fatter private sector pay packets to pursue their dream of making India self-sufficient in technology.

The best part of the experience is the sense of pride one got at the end of it. Nostalgically, I do recall the nine years spent working at Inmarsat in London as an NRI. Though I did not end up rich like Silicon Valley millionaires, money was never an issue. But taking up challenges was.

My sense of achievement stems from the fact that I contributed to changing the lives of millions of Indians and did not run after unscrupulous fame and fortune derived from manipulating the stock markets or other such petty actions. Making the country proud in terms of seeding its knowledge industry, to say the least, has indeed been ingratiating. It could not have been what it is today sans the sacrifices of some of us. If we did not make money, the country did. We created jobs from 40,000 to some millions today, we boosted exports from few millions to tens of billions, reported to be $60 billion this year. We were part of the revolution from 1991 onwards, when foreign exchange reserves had sunk to four weeks' supply.

I would like to spend the next part of my article specifically looking at some successes and failures that I had. I would also like to provide you an insight into the corporate world with some anecdotes.

Whether there were failures or successes, there have been defining moments like the GDR story, which failed in its first avatar but bounced back to success in the next one.

The other side of the coin were achievements like getting VSNL listed at LSE after two failed attempts, getting India to be a supplier of satellite capacity, bringing internet into India, and sharing a platform with Bill Gates in 1997. The fact that he expressed a desire to interact with me is a forgotten story.

The first failure was the devolvement of VSNL's global listing in 1994. This was to be the first by India, the first by a public sector undertaking and the biggest ever from India. It figured in the budget speech of 1994, by the then finance minister, Dr. Manmohan Singh. It shattered us all no end. We had worked hard and sincerely, but we had failed to deliver. Nonetheless, we pondered over and analysed the causes of the failures. The issue was re-launched with added vigour and it became a resounding success. It continued to be the biggest out of India until recently.

Yet another failure for me was not to get the government's nod for what I believed would make India the global hub for telecom, providing bandwidth on demand. It was a dream in 1992-93, when digital technology had really matured to be able to carry video, data, information and speech in one pipe.

Let me now move on to the insights of the corporate world.

Internet: Getting internet into India was purely driven by the realisation of the need for all communities to access information and knowledge and exchange ideas, information and knowledge at the speed of light. The commercial operations aptly started on 14th/15th August 1995. We were ahead of China. The headlines in the then press said, "Independence after 50 years." But the euphoria was short-lived. The service was pathetic due to poor market research and poor planning. The independence became a nightmare.

I admitted publicly that I had goofed. There was this bout of silence and look of pity directed at me. The APSU chief admitting his mistakes in public softened people's their approach on the issue and helped me win their hearts for a while. The press had headlines saying, "CMD VSNL says he goofed," but all was well in the end when the commitment was delivered.

There are a few more interesting bits to indicate what connectivity can do and has done.

One of VSNL's facilities is at a place called Narayangaon. The surrounding area produces the world's best grapes and bubbly wine. Those grapes could be seen at the shelves of Sainsbury in London with a line that said 'quality grapes from Narayangaon'. Frankly, there were tears in my eyes when I saw those products from the 'boondocks' of India on the shelves of Sainsbury's, one of the largest supermarket establishments in the world. This proved the power of connectivity

In another instance, I visited a shop at Jodhpur, called 'Maharani'. The shop sold its wares to the top shops on the high streets of London through the internet. It also facilitated exchange of designs and colours. This process, which took at least a dozen visits, was now getting completed in a dozen minutes. The best part was, when I gave my credit card after making purchases, the young lady owner of this big store asked me if I was the one who brought internet to India. I then understood how small the world was and how much smaller it could get.

Here is a small but interesting anecdote on delivery. There was this very smart minister of telecom, trade and industry from Israel, Ms Aloni. She was a guest at the Confederation of Indian Industry. I was to felicitate her and welcome her. In her speech, she talked about the inadequacies of the natural resources in Israel, except seawater. She said everything had to be imported. But I reminded her of what they had and we did not; they believed in not only doing but also managing and delivering. Doing is easy, but delivery is often painful. But it is also exhilarating. "You, Ms Aloni, believe more in delivery than just going over the motions of doing. Gentlemen, delivery is more important than going through the motions of doing. Commitment is beyond a promise. Promises one may break, but commitment has to be honoured. You all can take India to its past glory if you just ponder over this," I said.

The INSAT 2E deal: It was an experience of lifetime to get this $150-million deal through a board consisting of members from 20-odd countries, with US, UK and France leading the charge. I loved those behind-the-scene confabulations to convince 20-odd members of the board of the world body Intelsat to buy satellite capacity from India. The out-of-the-box ingenious thinking on the financial side, understanding concerns and addressing them on the human side, and advocating governments through our embassies on the diplomatic side was indeed an experience. All this did result in the final hurrah.

Life after VSNL

A few words on the private sector: This was an adjustment for me, after being in a place like VSNL. It was perhaps like having the thunder stolen from me a bit, as, in the private sector, one does not have the autonomy that one had in the public sector. The private companies are after your brand equity built over years and the intellectual capital you have accumulated. That talent could be retained, as I alluded to earlier, by following the seven tenets of authority, accountability audit, hire, fire, reward and rebuke. Once these are imparted, you can take decisions at the speed of light and compensate people for their performance while improving economic conditions and quality of life. The PSUs and institutes would certainly bounce back.

Finally, a concluding bit of advice. That was my tomorrow that I saw 60 years ago (yesterday) and knew little about. I have no regrets, just exhilarations of fulfilment. For those of you who aspire to be in my shoes or even bigger shoes in a few years' time, let me share with you some fundamental thoughts based on my experience here and later.

There are no shortcuts in life. The path ahead is tough, often difficult, and full of unknowns. The learning curve is steep. Therefore, getting rich quickly is not an ideal situation. It happens if it happens. But for lasting satisfaction, trying to get rich quick is not the truth; it is not the route or the ultimate reality. All of you are budding saplings. There will be brutal forces out there to crush you; there will be strong winds trying to blow you away. However, there are five basic principles I have followed that have helped me deal with the forces and winds, resulting in me being able to stand here today.

They are: honesty, integrity, hard work, sincerity/accountability, and commitment to deliver. Intending to do something is easy, but delivering it is often difficult and not without pain. But, when you do deliver, it is the most exhilarating experience one can have. Therefore, to be a winner, make sure you define your deliverables wherever you are and deliver them. In the process, you might have to re-assess, retreat and regroup for tactical reasons, but keep your eye on the main deliverables and go for the kill at the right time with renewed aggression. Deliver on time, as we did for the once devolved GDR issue of VSNL.

Along with these, one needs a few additional characteristics to survive successfully in the world outside. These are the ability to ride out one's luck to the best possible outcome (whether good or bad luck), the absolute belief in oneself as an immovable object in an ocean of unstoppable forces, and a good attitude towards life.

The tomorrow for you all is going to be tougher than what it had been for me, because of corruption-ridden polity, the bureaucracy, the systems and the materialist world. The system and the values are not what we lived with.

I am one of the very few to have been honoured as lifetime fellows. We have family scholarships in the name of our parents, totalling over 1 crore. About 150 students have benefitted from these. We top up every year by 5-6 lakh rupees. I also instituted a VSNL Chair in 1994, the first ever.

To the institute, I would say

I humbly pay my respects to my institute, my gurus, my parents, my friends/peers, superiors and my family for getting me to this stage.

Jai IIT Kharagpur, one of the temples of the present *yug*!

Mr. Syngal in his office

You Never Know When IIT Kharagpur Will Come to Your Rescue

Partha Sinha

1981-1986, B. Tech - Mechanical Engineering, Patel Hall, IIT Kharagpur

Partha Sinha joined the Times of India group as a president on the second day of the nationwide COVID lockdown. It was not just a healthcare crisis but it was a business crisis as well. There was no way the newspaper could be delivered to people's houses during a physical lockdown. This also meant there was no revenue. Parth was supposed to deliver the top line and lead a team of around 2,000 people at a time when the newspaper couldn't get to people's homes easily and he couldn't physically meet anybody from his team.

Today, after about a year and a half, the group is nearly out of the woods. Many of Parth's colleagues ask him how he was so confident about the recovery. He typically answers them with a smile, because, if he says, "IIT Kharagpur prepares you for everything," he may sound really smug. But the people who have been to IIT Kharagpur will know the truth.

It was always a black steel trunk and a bedding. Every student coming into IIT Kharagpur had to have these two lovely worldly possessions with them. It was almost like an identity badge. Many summers ago, on a hot sweltry afternoon, I got down at the Kharagpur station and looked around. I knew immediately who would catch a rickshaw from there and proceed to the cherished destination called Indian Institute of Technology. Of course, there were some distinctions and differentiations. The rich kids carried suitcases of the moulded variety. Some had their names properly stencilled on the black trunk. But a majority of people, like me, had just a handwritten label stuck on the trunk.

When we landed at the hostel, a few seniors met us at the gate and they were really polite—to me and my dad. I was wondering why I had heard of the monstrosity of IIT seniors and their ragging. After a couple of hours, my dad left for Kolkata and then life changed. Well, forever. The same seniors landed up in my room in the evening and that was pretty much the last time I saw my room during the ragging period.

"Hey freshie! Come here." This is the line that echoed in the corridors of Patel Hall over the next three weeks or so. All the seniors were trying to portray a menacing face. The freshers were scared to death. But I quickly figured out one thing—the power of storytelling.

I understood that the seniors were an academically inclined lot and wouldn't have had much luck with the fairer sex. They would have been too busy studying. I started telling everyone some concocted stories about the love lives of some of my friends from Kolkata. Everyone was lapping up these stories. With the exception of one or two strange people, nobody ragged me 'physically'. Stories have all the power. This is a much-touted idiom today. But IIT made me understand this very early in my life. And that is something I followed all my life. Creating a good narrative has helped companies I have worked with create a great brand, at times to get a great valuation or simply to become more relevant. Nowadays there are many storytellers and a lot of them are excellent. But thanks to the early days of IIT I can almost write a survivor's guide to storytelling. Understand your audience and create a story that will engage them— this is possibly the biggest learning of the corporate world today. I learnt it the hard way, during the ragging period at the toughest hostel in IIT Kharagpur.

The ragging period finished in a haze, and no there's no pun intended here. Before we realised, we were integrated into the mainstream of IIT life. Kharagpur became KGP and we were learning, imbibing and creating our own KGP lingo. Classes were going on in full swing and very soon I realised something to my horror. In my school, I was the academic dude and that was pretty much my identity. At KGP, everyone was an academic dude and this was not a differentiator anymore. The search for an identity started very soon. I didn't want to be an also-ran and I also didn't want to achieve my stripes through academics. Every single 18-year-old goes through this crisis at KGP and it is possibly one of the biggest learnings from IIT KGP. Finding your strength and your niche is a critical life lesson and I started learning it there the hard way. I started going for trials—from sports to dramatics and literary events. All the seniors (yes, the same ones who had ragged me a few weeks ago) were happily giving me advice and helping out. But soon I realised I had to do it on my own. For only you can find your own niche. Soon I could figure out that it would be literary activities for me. In four years, I could represent IIT several times and I finally passed out with a blue in literary activities.

The competitive world of debates and elocutions undoubtedly helped me in my life but what helped me the most was the lesson that one needs to find one's strength and start playing to it. Later on, whenever I have worked in large companies, I was always quick to find my niche. And here's a secret. Finding your own differentiated position in an organisation is far more rewarding than anything else. Thank you IIT KGP for those early days of identity crisis.

The most difficult part of writing anything about IIT KGP is probably the fact that one could get carried away. And there is a high chance of this. Describing the rich tapestry of images and experiences at IIT KGP needs a lot more words than what has been recommended to me.

Let me talk about two very significant challenges I had faced post my life at IIT KGP and how all the learnings at KGP had saved the day for me.

I wrote the CAT like most middle-class boys to get into the coveted management career. I didn't have much of an idea of management jobs except for the fact that they paid well. Anyway, I got called for interviews from all four of the IIMs—Ahmedabad, Calcutta (yes Calcutta and not Kolkata), Bangalore and Lucknow. We were told that the Ahmedabad interview would be the toughest one and it was nearly impossible to come out with flying colours. On the day of the interview, I was relieved to see a couple of other KGP people in the GD. The discussion started and the three of us dominated the discourse. We were from different batches, but KGP had given all three of us something unique—the ability to build on each other's arguments. At the end of the discussion, other candidates told us that domination was a very bad management trait and all three of us would be hugely penalised for that. But there was nothing much we could do about it at that time. Then it was time for the personal interview.

A very famous professor was in the panel, and he started shooting difficult questions right from the word go. In about a couple of minutes, I figured out that he was trying to bully me into submission. Now, here was a guy who had the experience of being ragged at the fabled Patel Hall at IIT KGP. How could he ever be bullied!? I kept my calm and told myself that there was no way the professor expected me to answer all those questions. Maybe he was trying to see how I responded to his aggression. I invoked everything I had learned during my ragging and faced him. And very soon he figured out that I wouldn't give up quickly. The interview went on for a while and I was kind of sure that I didn't get bullied. My feeling was validated a few weeks later when I was offered an admission at IIM Ahmedabad.

You never know how KGP comes to your rescue at difficult times!

And finally, something interesting about my current assignment. I joined the Times of India group as president on the second day of the nationwide Covid-19 lockdown. It was not just a healthcare crisis but, for me, more importantly, it was a business crisis. There was no way we could deliver the newspaper to people's houses during a physical lockdown. The whole country was gripped by fear, and nobody was getting the newspaper at home. This also meant there was no revenue. What a remarkable first day at work! I was supposed to deliver the top line and lead a team of around 2,000, at a time when our product couldn't get to people's homes, and I couldn't physically meet anybody from my team. Not just our organisation, but the entire corporate world had enough reasons to panic. But my mind travelled back a few decades. We were possibly in our second year when the entire contract staff of IIT KGP went on a strike. There was no food getting prepared at the hostels, nothing much was moving in the institute, and the trade union wanted to use the students as pawns to win the battle. So, what did the students do? They assured the institute that they would attend classes and write exams even if the entire contract staff went on a strike. Everyone thought that it was just bravado and we would all cave in. But we changed our way of living and ensured that all those duties were done by the students themselves. So, for a period of time, we were students-cum-contract-staff. Was it difficult? You bet it was!

But we knew we would rebuild normalcy in a different way. It could cause us some agony but eventually we would prevail. I was thinking exactly in the same manner when we faced the Covid crisis on the very first day of my joining the Times group. I knew that a legendary brand like the Times of India would find a way to navigate through this crisis. At that time, I had no idea what that way would be, and you can't really blame me since I was not even inducted into the business. But I was deliriously positive about the outlook. We went through an extremely difficult quarter. It not only accelerated my learning about the business, but it made the entire management team totally resolute that we would be able to come out of the crisis. A few months later, we were proven right and, today, after about a year-and-a-half, we are out of the woods.

Today, when many of my colleagues ask me how I was so confident about the recovery, when I didn't even know the realities of the business, I typically answer them with a smile. Because I am sure if I say, "IIT KGP prepares you for everything," I may sound really smug. Won't I? But the people who have been to IIT KGP will see the truth in it.

Chapter 4

Dancing to the Tune of Future: The Younger IITians

Gaurav Tripathi

Gaurav grew up moving across more than 10 cities, mostly in remote tribal areas, and finally landed in the big forest of IIT Bombay's campus. He is a 3x entrepreneur, moving through the highs and lows of start-up life. He is currently the founder and CEO of Superpro.ai. Gaurav has over 16 years of experience across multiple start-ups, working in the areas of web 2.0, video, IoT, cloud, big data, blockchain and AI. He has led a team to build an IP portfolio of over 120 patents (US/EU) in the areas around AI, of which 35 patents have him as an inventor. Gaurav enjoys trekking, travelling and reading.

Shreya Agrawal

The story of Shreya Agrawal is an extraordinary tale of a girl from Rajasthan who came to IIT Bombay for a PhD, four years after a master's degree, jobs in sales and marketing, and marriage. She found her passion in preventive healthcare during the six-year-stay on campus.

Today, Shreya is one of the directors of the IIT-B alumni association. She works as a freelance consultant and a wellness coach, conducting awareness sessions for various IT companies and NGOs. She also heads the R&D of a wellness brand called Aadar. She co-founded a unique venture called 'The Happy Collar'.

Nishant Jindal

This is an amazing story of a recent IIT-D graduate—Nishant Jindal's journey of persistence to get into IIT. His journey to IIT is highly inspirational to say the least. Getting into IIT-D is not all. In his story, Nishant describes the problems he faced academically and financially, the disillusionment he had, the issues about his future, his failed ventures/start-ups, and how he finally came out successful, ready to make a life of his dreams and take on the world.

Akanksha Swarnim

Akanksha Swarnim belongs to Pusa in Bihar, a small university town. In Kharagpur she met students from all over India and her perspective broadened. At IIT Kharagpur, she got an opportunity to go to Hong Kong in her fourth year for internship. It was the first time that she travelled alone abroad. This was a big accomplishment for a girl from a small place and it made her mother very proud. Her biggest takeaway from Kharagpur was the confidence it instilled in her—so that she could stand on her own legs and make a difference. She was able to observe and understand different types of challenges in different aspects of life around her. In Gurgaon, she came to know about Upay, a footpath *pathshala* concept. This changed her life.

From childhood, Akanksha had been a person with great empathy. Whenever she saw youngsters at the traffic lights, crossing the road with begging bowls in hand, she had an urge from within to help them. She felt secure financially and in all other ways, but she wanted to do more—something useful to society. Akanksha started searching on the internet about opportunities to do volunteer community work. Soon she came to know about Varun Srivastava, the founder of Upay, and learned that he was also from IIT Kharagpur.

Akanksha runs four centres in Gurgaon and three centres in NCR. Each centre has 50 to 60 children. She found that the children were not only intelligent but also highly motivated to learn. This gave her immense satisfaction. She could feel the change happening. As a result of this work, she found life more meaningful.

The Friends I Made, Made Me

Gaurav Tripathi

2001-2005, Aerospace Engineering, Hostel 5, IIT Bombay

> *Gaurav grew up moving across more than 10 cities, mostly in remote tribal areas, and finally landed in the big forest of IIT Bombay's campus. He is a 3x entrepreneur, moving through the highs and lows of start-up life. He is currently the founder and CEO of Superpro.ai. Gaurav has over 16 years of experience across multiple startups, working in the areas of web 2.0, video, IoT, cloud, big data, blockchain and AI. He has led a team to build an IP portfolio of over 120 patents (US/EU) in the areas around AI, of which 35 have him as an inventor. Gaurav enjoys trekking, traveling and reading.*

It was the mid-90s. I was in Grade 8 or 9. We were living in Rajnandgaon where my father, a constable in the Chhattisgarh police, was posted. We had recently shifted to this place and I was a new entrant to a school where other students had been studying together since Grade 1. Naturally, I found it difficult to make friends.

Added to this was a huge mismatch of aspirations. Ambitions for most people around me didn't go beyond wanting to be a truck driver. I became a recluse and found solace in my books and studies.

But, for some reason unknown to me till date, another guy from school got talking to me. While others treated me like an outsider, this boy extended a hand of friendship. When he realised that I was good at academics, he started enrolling me for inter-school competitions. He would fill the form, pay the fees and just inform me that I had to be present at a certain place on a certain day.

Once such event was a state-level general knowledge competition organised by ABVP. As always, I participated on this guy's insistence. And I won the second place. There was a big award ceremony to which parents were invited. I was conferred the title of 'Chhattisgarh Shri' along with a cash prize of 2000 rupees. This was more than my father's salary at that time! Winning this award was an undoubted proof for my father that his son was good at studies and should be encouraged to study further.

This incident was a turning point for me in many ways. First, it truly taught me what friendship meant. And, secondly, it cemented the importance of excelling academically.

Early life

I was born in Varanasi in 1983 in a big joint family. Circumstances had forced my father to abandon his studies to run the family. He moved to Jabalpur in search of a job. That's when he got recruited as a constable in the Madhya Pradesh police.

Being in the police force meant frequent relocations to remote destinations. Leaky roof and irregular water supply became a part of our lives, as did finding a solution to each of these problems.

Each location we moved to also brought with it unique learnings. Having hardcore street fighters as peers in the densely forested Mandla area taught me to be street smart. Kanker was where I saw mountains for the first time in my life. I learnt to cycle up the hill, differentiate between poisonous and non-poisonous snakes, and identify a bear's trail by following its poop!

This is also where I flourished as a student. I had been a good student all along but here I was appreciated for being one. I still remember receiving my first-ever book, *Jungle Book*, as a gift from my sister Jyoti.

Some of my lifelong friendships were forged here. Nilimp was the son of the jailor here. Even though we were quite different from each other, we became good friends. The friendship outlasted our time together in Kanker. Even today, he is my best friend.

Getting into IIT

I heard of this place called the IIT for the first time from Nilimp. I was in Grade 8 and Nilimp's uncle had gotten into IIT Kanpur. This was something big is all I knew back then. I started studying for IIT right after Grade 10. IIT Kanpur (the only one I knew) was far and hence out of reach, I had concluded till then.

But, after winning the Chhattisgarh Shri, the topic of IIT and engineering cropped up again. This time I gave it a serious thought and decided to shift to Bhilai to attend the coaching classes for IIT entrance. It meant staying alone for the first time in my life. My father supported me wholeheartedly, making the transition easier.

I couldn't get into the most sought-after classes. I didn't have enough money to pay the expected fees too. But, by then, the dream of getting into IIT was set in my mind. I am grateful that the teachers saw the sincerity in me and agreed to coach me.

That year turned out to be the most successful year for our class, with four students getting through IIT entrance. I was the highest ranked student among them.

My counselling was at IIT Bombay. The moment I set my foot into the IIT Bombay campus, I fell in love with it. But there was a twist awaiting me. My family had moved to Varanasi and my father heard that I could easily get into BHU, Varanasi. "That's perfect," he said. It would cut down our expenses as I could stay with the family itself.

I reluctantly moved to the BHU campus. But something was amiss. I had to find a way to get into IIT Bombay. Without letting anyone at home know, I appeared for the entrance exams again. Thankfully, there weren't any twists this time. The road led straight to IIT Bombay.

Entrepreneurial journey

The year was 2001, with the Mumbai monsoon in full swing. While I was excited to be in IIT Bombay, life on campus was nothing short of a cultural shock for me. Most exchanges were in English, a language I was barely comfortable in at that time.

When I heard of *Insight*, the campus newspaper, my first reaction was, "Why would the campus have only an English newspaper?" It just didn't seem right. Why was there no regional language paper on a campus that had students from all corners of India? Why not start a Hindi newspaper?

But I wasn't the only one with this question. There was one more at least. My friend Gunjan was already thinking a step ahead. And so it began. We got a few more like-minded students, mostly the ones with a similar background, facing a culture shock just like me. Our batchmates ridiculed us and even labelled us 'attention seekers' and 'problem creators'. What is this 'anti-establishment' attitude, we were asked.

While the excitement levels were high, the practical stuff still had to be sorted out. Where would we print the paper? What software would we to use to make the layout? We didn't even know that we needed the dean's permission for such an activity!

But, eventually, we managed to get the required permissions and approvals, including the budget. Logistics was taken care of with a bicycle; night time was used for distribution.

Thus began *Awaaz*, the Hindi newspaper at the IIT Bombay campus, which runs even today, a couple of decades later. I didn't know at that time that the first seeds of my entrepreneurial journey had been sown. And yes, the newspaper also marked the start of a timeless friendship with Gunjan.

Meanwhile, I had also participated in the hostel elections. I stood for the post of social secretary; it was the first ever election of my life. In spite of my arrogance, my friends and seniors ensured a thumping victory for me. My main responsibility as social secretary was to figure out a way to do whatever needed to be done! From finding guys to do women's roles in plays to getting winning participants for a dance competition, I did it all. And I did it rather successfully. That's when I realised that I might be good at something, after all.

The most enriching experience of my IIT days was with *Ethos*, a magazine. My friend Gopi Vikranth approached me with the idea to do something on the lines of *MIT Tech Review* at IIT. Over 300 students across the 7 IIT campuses enrolled themselves into the idea of *Ethos*. We also reached out to the IIT alumni and gathered a lot of support.

We contacted Ambi Parmeshwar, an IIT-M alumnus, the founder of the top ad agency FCB Ulka for the branding and logo of *Ethos*. He was impressed by our boldness to just walk up to him and ask for help. He agreed to be a part of it. Ajit Balakrishnan, the CEO of the Rediff portal, used to visit our campus frequently for lectures. He assured us of his backing. The team at Rediff even helped us get online, which was an uncommon feat back in 2004. We had even spoken to Mr Jairam Ramesh, an IIT Bombay alumnus about *Ethos* and the backing that it had received.

But we could not bring all the different stakeholders on the same page and eventually we had to give up on the idea of *Ethos*. The difference between what was and what could have been was disappointing.

Around the same time, Prof Anil Gupta of IIM Ahmedabad, who had heard of our efforts with *Ethos*, got in touch with me. He wanted to get the project work or thesis in the IIT libraries out in the public domain. We took up the task of scanning them right away. But word got out, and all hell broke loose. We were told that this would lead to IP infringement issues. We were told to stop the work immediately. I argued that this was public property and should be available to everyone. But it was a lost cause. We had to give it up.

By this time, I had managed to buy a computer for myself. With the meagre RAM and hard disk space that I could afford, Windows couldn't run on my system. Furthermore, my roommate Chinmay (who had become the hostel's computer secretary) used to hack my PC regularly. Thanks to his antics, I shifted to Linux. And it felt like I had entered a whole new realm. This was my introduction to the world of programming and creation. Linux, to me, became an expression of technology and power.

Meanwhile, I had become a regular at the lectures conducted at the School of Management. I attended lectures by the likes of Randy Komisar, Narayan Murthy and other giants. When I asked Mr Murthy what was the best time to start a business, his instant reply was, "Now." These lectures and interactions made a huge impact on me.

By then the start-up bug had bitten me. I also saw a few of my seniors leave their good jobs and choose to start something on their own.

Entrepreneurial journeys

To start anything, I could not ask my family or friends for money. I had to figure out a way to make money. During 2003-05, LAN gaming had become really big in the campus and a lot of students had started buying PCs for gaming. I sensed an opportunity here. Lamington Road in Mumbai became my favourite hangout. Soon, with a couple of friends, I was assembling and selling powerful computer systems to the first generation of gamers at the IIT campus.

Selling assembled computers taught me that there was a lot of money to be made. When I heard that the entire batch of the management school was planning to buy laptops, I decided to pitch in. I assured them powerful configurations, parts from Singapore and competitive prices. They had done their homework and had heard good things about us. "Where's your office?" they asked us. We were still operating out of the campus. But we couldn't tell them that. We printed visiting cards with an address that we had no office in. "It's still being made," was a white lie we had to resort to. They agreed.

Later, the management students did realise that the laptops hadn't been imported by us really and we simply traded in laptops. But since they did work well and we had got them a better deal, there was nothing to complain about. They did, however, comment that though they had enrolled for a business management course, we were the ones who had shown them how to do business. This gave us the confidence that we could make money.

Looking back, I can also see my first mistake running a business—we didn't think of it as a business even when I was making money. We had only looked at it as fundraising for doing 'something else'. Had we known better, we could and would have scaled this business.

But what's an entrepreneur's journey without a massive dose of learnings!

We eventually shifted to a more appropriate office at Kailash Industrial Estate, right behind the campus. Kailash Industrial Estate would soon become the start-up hub of Powai—a place where most entrepreneurial journeys that began on campus would set up offices. It gives me immense pleasure that we were the ones to lead this pack.

My focus now shifted to what was, in my mind, a 'real' business idea. We decided to build an equivalent to YouTube in India. But the funding problem persisted. This time, Shekhar Kulkarni, another IIT alumnus, came to our rescue. I had met him during the IIT days. He had himself started a venture in Pune and was bullish about creating techpreneurs in India. He became our first angel investor, a term I hadn't yet learnt.

We began building this platform. But soon reality struck. "Step out of Powai and look at the real world a little," Ajit Balakrishnan told us. He was right. The internet speeds prevalent in India were so low that YouTube couldn't be used effectively.

We eventually got an exit and a part of the team was acquired/hired by another start-up, which got acquired by one of the largest players in online entertainment at that time.

No other team in India had done the kind of work in video and technology that we had done. But, at the time, the importance of this work was lost on us.

Soon after, I got married and moved to Pune. I started doing some work in the software development services sector, which was flourishing after the 2008 recession. My mentor and my earlier angel investor, Shekhar, helped me settle in Pune. I always had the itch to build technology products in India.

In Germany

The year was 2011 and my old friend Gunjan called me to say that he wanted to start something with me. My initial reaction was to tell him no and ask him to continue with his job at BCG in Germany. But he insisted; so I asked him to resign first and then call me. A month later he told me that he had put in his papers. Now we had to start.

The result was Innoplexus, a life sciences AI company, which uses AI to help top pharmaceutical companies across the world cut down their time and effort in drug development by generating insights from their data. We chose to do it the conventional bootstrapped way and made it into what became India's first profitable AI company. We got into Big Pharma at the right time when they were still sceptical about emerging technologies. We saw a lot of highs and lows; we were almost bankrupt in between but team spirit was our strength.

We could not raise funds in India and had to move to Germany where we were able to raise multiple rounds of funding. This was a big leap from the early days of not knowing what angel investment meant.

We ended up being known as 'Google of Life Sciences' in Europe and our team members are still one of the most sought after by any company working in AI. As the co-founder and CTO there, I led the team, which filed 120+ patents across US and Europe, around different areas like computer vision, natural language processing, ontologies, entity recognition and blockchain.

We had a number of Fortune 500 companies as our clients, including some of the largest pharmaceutical companies in the world. Innoplexus is still going strong with its headquarters in Germany and I continue to be on its board in Germany.

I led an industrial delegation from Germany to Gujarat to promote FDI in Gujarat.

Gaurav Tripathi with the Prime Minister of India, Narendra Modi, and Mr Wolfgang Schuster, Lord Mayor of Stuttgart, Germany on a very successful mission to promote FDI from Germany in Gujarat.

Back to India

While travelling across the world, I got to experience a phenomenon I hadn't experienced before in India. Even the common man abroad was concerned about who controlled the data that they was being created online, which app had access to what data, and what were they doing with the data.

India, by then, had already the largest user base on almost all the big foreign apps. What is happening to all the data that is being created by these Indian users? Does India have any control over these apps or the massive data that is being created?

It soon became apparent that the answer to all these questions is negative. In that case, what lies ahead for India? I believe India needs a more Indian tech ecosystem with control being more with Indian entities to ensure India does not end up being a modern data colony.

This is what led me to start another start-up while still with Innoplexus.

I am now the co-founder and CEO of Superpro.ai. Superpro builds software products around communication data and AI. It is backed by prominent Indian investors like IvyCap SUSV and MOX PENTHALON ventures. Its mission includes ensuring the company's technological and data sovereignty. Superpro aims to make it easy for businesses to adopt to the new future of work and engage better with clients, customers, investors and other stakeholders.

The world has changed and so has the way we work. We no longer need to be in the office to do our jobs. Work is more fulfilling for us as individuals if we are able to be with our families and friends and in places where we want to be.

Along with Innoplexus, I continue to forge ahead with Superpro.ai. These are two of my most successful start-ups to date.

As Steve Jobs said, you can connect the dots only looking backwards. Every stage of my life taught me something and helped me take a step forward. But, foremost, at every step I was fortunate enough to get help from friends. Whether it is Gunjan coming as a founder, Gopi coming in as an investor, Arunabh connecting me to my current co-founders or Kunal (my hostel senior and founder of Flipspaces) designing our first office and many more such instances, I can say for sure that I could not have reached this far without the friends I made in the campus. And for me, that is the best gift I got from my days on campus.

Lastly, I wish to say that things were much easier for our generation of IITians, whether it was looking for a job, finding investments for start-ups and all other respects. The IIT brand had been established and been put on a solid foundation by the earlier batches of students from the 60s, 70s and 80s, who went through difficult times but still managed to give IIT its brand name, image and credibility. For this we remain grateful to them.

That Purple Road:
My Memoir of IIT Bombay

Dr. Shreya Agrawal

2011-2017, PhD, Centre for Research in
Nano Technology and Science, IIT-B

The story of Shreya Agrawal is an extraordinary tale of a girl from Rajasthan who came to IIT Bombay for PhD, four years after a master's degree, jobs in sales and marketing and marriage. She found her passion in preventive healthcare during the six-year-stay on campus.

Today, Shreya is one of the directors of the IIT-B alumni association. She works as a freelance consultant and a wellness coach, conducting awareness sessions for various IT companies and NGOs. She also heads the R&D of a wellness brand called Aadar. She co-founded a unique venture called 'The Happy Collar'.

My journey to IIT

Let me time travel to circa 2007. I had always aspired to become an IAS officer, nothing less, nothing more. But perhaps destiny had some other plans for me.

In July 2007, after finishing my M. Sc. in biotechnology from another city of dreams, Kota, I got a chance to visit Mumbai for the first time for the admission of my brother Harsh at IIT Bombay.

I remember, when our taxi entered the lush green campus near Powai Lake, a gush of non-polluted, sweet and cool air touched my face and the scenic views of IIT started rolling in front of my eyes. The vast playgrounds, the convocation hall, the gardens, the administrative buildings, and the hostels on the way immediately captivated me to the core.

I was secretly admiring the fortune and brawn of IIT students and perhaps I wished to be a part of that institute. But I never knew this dream was going to come true.

Somewhere in October the same year, I got selected for job training with Lifecare Innovations in Gurgaon and got a posting in Mumbai. On the very day I landed in Mumbai, I fell in love with the city. It was like love at the first step.

Well, in 2011, after clearing the UGC (University Grants Commission) National Eligibility Test, securing an all-India rank of 155, I started applying for PhD in various IITs. I applied for a PhD in IIT Kanpur and IIT Kharagpur, apart from IIT Bombay.

While filling the PhD application form of IIT-B, I ticked the Department of Biosciences as per my academic background, where interviews were scheduled on 2nd May. I was sure that I would clear the interview in this department, though there was one more department I was eligible to apply in—the Centre for Research in Nanotechnology and Science (CRNTS). The date for this was 6th May.

As I had already chosen my preference, according to my academic background, I didn't feel the need to fill in the other option. But, after a while of mental turmoil, I just ticked the other choice too.

Who knew at that moment that CRNTS would emerge as a saviour in the interview season and that one small tick in front of 'CRNTS' would change my life forever!

It was 2nd May 2011. I was curled up in the sleeper seat of a private bus somewhere in the countryside of Bharuch, Gujarat. As the clock ticked 4 am, I woke up startled by the loud ring from my phone. It was my mom calling to inquire about my whereabouts.

To my shock and dismay, I found that the bus had halted for service in the wee hours and it would take a few hours for the bus to become functional. We were still more than 300 km away from Mumbai where I had to report at 8 am for a PhD interview at the biosciences department of the Indian Institute of Technology Bombay.

Restless and clueless, I got the order from my mom to hitchhike and reach Mumbai somehow. Sleepy and anxious, I deboarded the bus as my worried mother kept frantically calling my brother and her friends. In the pitch dark, in the early hours of the morning, with all my luggage, I walked along the highway waiting for some vehicle that could lead me to Mumbai. After half an hour of trying to find a 'safe' vehicle, I finally boarded a bus, securing a little space to tuck myself outside the driver's cabin.

I asked my brother, who was studying in IIT-B at that time, to inform the person concerned about my delay due to unavoidable circumstances.

After reaching Borivali in that godsent vehicle, I took a rickshaw to Powai and reached the campus around 9 am. I unpacked my bag at the temporary stay at the girls' hostel #11 and got ready for the interview. I was sleep-deprived and nervous and had a super foggy brain as I walked towards the Department of Biosciences and Bioengineering to appear for my first PhD interview ever.

IIT-B, here I come

As expected, I could not recall half the answers and the rest of the answers were lost somewhere in the topsy-turvy and adventurous journey of the previous night.

I met their questions with incorrect/partially correct answers and blank stares. Finally, referring to my last work experience (viz. sales and marketing), one of the panellists mockingly said that they would call me if IIT Bombay ever needed a marketing person.

For a few minutes, I could not even understand whether he was praising me or asking me to leave. Well, I mustered the courage to smile and headed towards the exit, embarrassed and disheartened.

I was absolutely discouraged to take up any more PhD interviews. I had already applied for PhD at IIT Kharagpur and IIT Kanpur and was planning to apply for IIT Delhi.

Well, I came back with a long face to the hostel. Then suddenly an ambrosial fragrance of Swarn Champa, aka Sonchhafa flowers, entered my nostrils, immediately refreshing me with new hopes and a lively mood. I was filled with gratitude towards my temporary roommate Pradnya, who had kept the flowers on her table, filling the room with fresh calmness. Since that day, those flowers have a special place in my heart.

The next morning, as I woke up relaxed, I vividly remembered how my heart longed to live in that campus as the morning breeze from the flowery thickets near Powai Lake touched my room's window. It was pure bliss, and that heavenly feeling made me feel at home, instantly.

After four days, on 6th May 2011, I had to appear for an interview at a different department—CRNTS.

As the hangover of 2nd May continued, I had the least interest to prepare or perform at this interview. Also, the thought of staying away from family for over five years was making me feel distressed and I secretly wished I would not get selected. It was my better half Vineet who convinced me to have faith in my abilities and give my best shot. His support through the ups and downs of my PhD programme was phenomenal. It would have been impossible to achieve the PhD milestone without Vineet, my super-cool parents and my in-laws.

Vineet insisted that I appear for the interview as I was anyway in the campus and it would at least 'add' to my experience. So, here I was, composed and carefree, as I had no expectation or desire to clear the interview.

Upon entering the interview room, I saw four panellists. I greeted them all and took my seat. The usual part began with questions from immunology, molecular biology and so on. I was super cool in the interview. I could easily recall the answers. Moreover, I immediately confessed my ignorance for the questions that I couldn't answer rather than ponder over them or frame an answer out of the blue.

Here comes the funny part. Somehow, this cocktail of cool head and honesty worked in my favour in both the rounds of the interview.

Voila! After a few days, on 23rd May, I got the interview result from CRNTS. My name was on the top of the list of less than 10 selected students. Suddenly, I felt the dream of joining IIT was finally coming true.

After some pondering over whether to take it up or not, I concluded that this golden opportunity should not be missed and that I must go ahead and prepare for the new phase of my life.

My life and times at IIT-B

Well, after confirmation from CRNTS, a few weeks of preparation and planning, I packed my bags and arrived at the IIT-B campus for admission, where a lot of formalities needed to be completed—hostel allocation, bank account, ID card, mess card, department enrolment and umpteen other processes, along with meetings with the supervisor and co-supervisor.

The happiness of being in such a beautiful campus was beyond words. It was a place where butterflies whirled, fireflies sparkled in the monsoon, birds flocked, mangoes dropped, and endless seasonal jamuns splashed about, painting the roads purple. It was the place where hills, lakes, ponds, gardens, a variety of trees and flowers adorned the breezy mornings and chilly evenings.

Initially, I got a microfluidics-related project upon joining. Though I didn't like it much, I thought I should give it a try and go ahead. I joined Prof Sameer Jadhav and Prof Shamik Sen, as it was a mandate at CRNTS to have two guides from two different departments.

After a few months, I approached the head of the department for changing my project but, as a rule, this was discouraged. I was advised to continue my work and tune into it, at least for the next six months to a year. I still did not sync with the project and decided to go through the vagaries of changing projects. It meant changing the guide, the co-guide and the lab. Rushing from applications and e-mails to calls and committees and meeting various professors, it was no less than a nightmare to go through this transition in the middle of a PhD programme.

But, finally, I could change my project to something themed around herbal extracts and their use with nanocarriers for orthopaedic applications (under Prof Rohit Srivastava and Prof Dhirendra Bahadur). I had the relentless encouragement and support of my friends and family.

Added to this travail was the qualifier exam. The HoD announced that this special exam was compulsory, wherein papers of engineering maths and statistics had to be cleared to retain the validity of admission. The students were quite agitated but there was no option and we all started studying. We caught hold of our genius mathematics friends and took off from practical lab work.

I felt literally numb at this announcement as I had always wanted to escape maths as a subject. I was always got thrashed for being poor at numbers; they never seemed to make much sense to me. I had never picked up a maths book after Grade 10, as I was free to take biology along with chemistry and physics. But it seemed mathematics loved me way too much and it encountered me in the form of this exam. After three exam attempts and 1.5 years, the department realised that it was not serving any purpose and the rule was finally suspended, after wasting many precious months.

Hostel life was zestful and super comfortable. At the girls hostel #10, I changed six accommodations in six years. The seventh floor room of hostel #10 had the best view from the window, overlooking canopies of tall trees and the shining waters of Powai Lake. I could spend hours sitting by the window.

There used to be a lot of roles and positions of responsibility for mess, maintenance, sports, academics and music, to name a few. In 2013, I got a chance to stand for the position of mess councillor (Mess Co). With the love and support of my hostelites, I bagged that role and tried my luck at changing the food options at the hostel to healthier versions, such as sweets with no artificial colours and flavours, soups without thickening agents, and so on, as wellness had always been a subject of my interest. I was also against wasting food. I recollect one of my friends capturing my photograph from a distance while I was feeding leftovers to the cows near the lake during that period.

IIT-B gave me a lot of cultural exposure during my stay. I was blessed to win three competitions at the PG cultural event (March 2012), which culminated in the award of 'Gem of PG Culturals'.

I was lucky to nurture my hobbies of theatre, fashion shows, Hindi composition, singing, and dance to name a few. All those years, I kept participating in various events. My most favourite moments are from anchoring the shows of Pandit Hari Prasad Chourasia ji, Kumar Vishwas and Pandit Vishwa Mohan Bhatt, in Hindi, and hosting *Surbahar* and *Swarsandhya*, the two evergreen musical nights of IIT-B that take place every year.

In dramatics, one of the most memorable roles is that of Sakku Bai, played by me in a play for the Main Drama General Championships, aka MDGC, an inter-hostel event. Sakku Bai was a loquacious, vibrant and chirpy maid from a Mumbai suburb, in this play called *Shobhana Tai*. I still remember how she kept gossiping with her *maalkin*, with rolling eyes, a naughty grin, one hand on her waist and the other one holding a broom across the shoulder.

I reminisce how it was so difficult for me to stop talking in Sakku Bai's *Bambaiya* accent for months together! I may have stepped down the stage that night but a figment of Sakku Baai still manages to live in me—happy in her own playfulness!

I was fortunate to have my younger brother Harshvardhan around. He was a dual-degree student of mechanical engineering. He was also the first secretary) of the movie club *Silverscreen* and was also super active in the photography club and other arts.

Even with the normal probability of finding a student in the same campus, I saw my brother only twice (of course without a plan to meet). I still wonder how he always managed to evade from my sight!

Academics and culturals would have been equally incomplete without my two buddies whom I met on campus—Bhushan N. Kharbikar and Ajay V. Suryavanshi. We met for cultural and academic reasons, went on to become lab mates, besties and eventually we three shared a bond that everybody wished to be a part of. Our group was called SAB (Shreya, Ajay, Bhushan). As 'SAB' means 'all', we never needed anything else once we were together. One was super frolicsome, always ready to dance, and the other one always up for serious discussions on history, science, technology and whatnot!

We three complemented each other so well that people around us dreamt of being part of such a great tribe. Our celebrations, taking care of each other in tough times, studying and experimenting together, travelling together... everything was just out of the world! Even the sequence of our pre-synopsis presentation and defence presentation was in the sequence of S-A-B.

On the experimental front, there was a lot that I learned—from handling an electron microscope to writing grant applications. After successfully developing two biomaterials that I worked on, finally in August 2017, I 'convocated' with my besties, holding memories for a lifetime and a second home called 'Insti'.

In 2021, I got the rare opportunity as a member of the board of directors of the IIT Bombay Alumni Association. It is said that I was the quickest to join the board after graduation and one of the youngest members of the board. I had always dreamt of doing something significant for this goldmine called IIT-B and I hope to make the best of it.

A dream fulfilled

IIT Bombay has given me a lifetime of lessons and reasons to grow, celebrate, learn, and help the world be a better place.

The place taught me about life, it is the place where hills and lakes exist, it is the place that is equally welcoming to one and all. It is the place that has my heart, forever.

So...

From 2011 to 2017...

From failed interviews to topping the charts...

From being a 'Nabdu' to being a 'Stud'...

From flying to London with a broken leg to changing guides...

From being overwhelmed with obnoxious chemicals at 2 am to having *dosas* at 4 am...

From strolling along the lakeside road with buddies to protesting in front of the director's office...

From teaching slum kids to climbing slippery hills...

From getting nervous backstage to meeting celebrities in annual fests...

From giving last-minute seminars to preserving experimental rabbits...

From giving instructions to cook to getting scolded by the department head...

From feeding leftover *chapatis* to crows on the terrace to sharing besties' tiffin...

From learning Marathi to forgetting high-school lessons...

From attending campus weddings to painting roads at midnight...

From Salsa classes to Kalamkari sessions...

From picking fresh mangoes from the roadside to teaching yoga on the hostel rooftop...

From being a fresher to a board member of the alumni association...

From admission counter to convocation hall...

From student card to alumni card...

From strangers to families and from formal grins to heartfelt smiles,

Life happened.

I bow in front of my cosmos of bliss and wisdom. *Gyanam paramam dhyeyam.* (Knowledge is the supreme goal.)

Getting into IIT and Getting through It

Nishant Jindal

2016-2021 Mechanical Engineering IIT Delhi

> *This is an amazing story of persistence of Nishant Jindal to get into IIT. His journey to IIT Delhi is highly inspirational to say the least. Getting into IIT-D is not all. In his story, Nishant describes the problems he faced academically and financially, the disillusionment he had, the issues about his future, his failed ventures/start-ups, and how he finally came out successful, ready to make a life of his dreams and take on the world.*

I got to know how the prestigious IITs came into being from Jain Uncle (Mr Davender Jain). To my amazement, he was from one of the earliest batches of IIT. The IITs were not as majestic back then. We, the 21st-century IITians, benefit enormously from the legacy that these eminent men have created. It is due to these high achievers, the men with nerves of steel, that we feel that being IITians we can reach any height on the face of the earth.

IITs are the most coveted institutes everywhere in this nation. The opportunities that the IITs provide are unparalleled. When I was preparing for JEE, youngsters were being attracted to the IITs after hearing about the big packages that IITians got. Nowadays, IIT aspirants are also fascinated by the large number of unicorn start-ups that IIT has created.

Reaching IIT per se is one definition of success in India. Of course, 1.5 million students have started trying their luck and might in JEE, the entrance exam of IIT. Today, students start preparing for it since the sixth class. Yes, that's an astounding seven-year preparation!

How did I make it to IIT?

My father came from the Kaithal district in Haryana. Back in the early days, a bus ride from Kaithal to Delhi cost a few rupees. My father's financial situation was such that he abstained from buying any food item en route to Delhi to save money. In 1999, when I was born, he worked very hard at his newly opened small general store in Delhi. He was an ambitious man. In 2004, 24-carat gold cost ₹5850. It was unthinkable to pay ₹1772 per month just for school fees. He didn't study beyond primary level but he wanted his child to get the best education.

However, I did not have any family legacy in education to follow. I didn't even know that homework was meant to be done. I knew so little English that when the teacher said, "It's the last warning," I thought she meant that if I did not obey her it would be my last morning on this planet.

Years kept passing by, and I remained average. My father considered funding my education as his puja. He enthusiastically made me attempt many Olympiads and exams. But never did I show any result. Once, at a prize distribution ceremony in my school, the names of awardees were being called out. My father was dismayed that I was not in the list. He said to me, "*Mere kaantarasgaye. Tera naam hi nahisunayidiya.*" (My ears kept yearning to hear your name, but your name wasn't called out.) After putting years of effort into me, he saw no results.

After tenth class, I took science and joined a JEE coaching centre. Now I was competing with millions, many of whom had been preparing for five years already and only 10k would reach IIT. Generally, JEE aspirants enrol themselves in 'non-attending' schools to get maximum time for JEE preparation. Having no one to guide me, I went to a regular school. Despite the hefty fee the coaching centre charged, the training provided by it was substandard.

The year was 2014. I had a small study room. We had one air-conditioner; it was installed in my room. We had one Scooty and it was given to me.

Time was flying fast. I just had two years for my preparation. The mornings were wasted in school, where the studies weren't so rigorous from a JEE standpoint. The evenings were wasted at the coaching centre. The rest of the time was wasted doing mundane homework for school. There was no time to study for JEE. When I had wasted almost 1.5 years of my preparation time, I thought I was out of the race altogether.

But then, a series of events happened that overturned my JEE aspiration and consequently my life. An organic chemistry lecture was going on in the coaching institute. Suddenly, a bearded man barged in and shouted out some names. It was the list of students whose fees were due. My name was also on that list. I was withheld from attending classes. I returned home early that day. My father admonished me for returning early. I explained everything to him. He had been suffering from rheumatoid arthritis for many years. He had to shut down his shop due to immense pain and swelling in his limbs and joints. He was very sick that day, with his face red due to fever. But he quickly picked up his cheque book and rushed to the coaching centre.

En route, I told him, "Dad, the coaching centre is not worth paying so much money. I would rather study by myself. We have already paid them a lot to no avail." He replied, "Today, I will arrange the funds somehow, but later, I do not want to hear from you that 'my father didn't have money, so I could not succeed'." His reply made the 16-year old in me speechless. I could not stop him from paying the fees. He signed three cheques—one for ₹50,000 dated the next day, another for ₹23,000 dated one month later, and another for ₹22,000 dated two months later.

The next morning, he borrowed money on interest and deposited it in the bank. This event was shocking. I realised my father's *tapasya*. My education was his life's purpose. That moment urged me to take tough decisions. I started spending money like water—on books and resources. I stopped going to school and the coaching centre.

I studied 16 hours a day for four months non-stop—I read thick books, did rigorous problems, pored over mathematics, did visualisation, took mock tests taking whatnot! By and by, my syllabus got completed. By then I had gained so much confidence that even if I had performed my worst, I would have been way above the threshold to reach the IITs.

May 22, 2016—the D day, the IIT JEE day

In that six-hour-long exam, most of the problems were rigorous and way beyond manageable. But I knew that I had only one chance; so I kept crawling on that rough road for six hours. Later, I got to know that, despite scoring only 60%, I had bagged an all-India rank of 247, from among more than a million aspirants. It was because the paper was the toughest ever in the history of JEE Advanced!

My five years of B. Tech

At last, I reached IIT Delhi and chose mechanical engineering. We, as JEE aspirants, are often told that reaching IIT sets up our life. Most of us young aspirants equate reaching IIT to salvation. So far, IIT had been the ultimate goal for me, but then, I was in a crisis. I wondered, *I have reached IIT. What next now?*

I had no motivation to study at IIT Delhi. So I just spent my time socialising, online and offline. Besides, I began writing about my JEE experiences on the internet. My posts got viral and I soon became the most popular IIT JEE mentor. My tips were relatable to millions.

I started providing home tuitions in South Delhi. I earned a decent amount of money. I even saved money.

My entry to IIT was glorious. I was the highest ranker at IIT Delhi to take up mechanical engineering. I was the centre of attention. However, it didn't take much time for the glory to fade out. I became insignificant. I saw my peers performing well in academics, research and projects, whereas I was just a tutor. I became a six-pointer after three semesters. To me, it seemed as though I had lost almost all the opportunities that IIT offered by spoiling my chances at academics.

Then a thought struck my mind, *Civil services is considered a reputable career among IITians. I have cracked one exam with flying colours. Why can't I crack another? The success in the civil services exam is independent of one's CGPA. Furthermore, after cracking it, I would be at par with my peers.*

So I joined a civil services coaching centre in my fourth semester. I proudly paid for the training using my own earnings from tutoring. I was performing well. My life had a purpose. I was passionate, motivated and focused again.

Unfortunately, years of following a sedentary lifestyle afflicted me with severe backache. At one point, it became unbearable. I started hitting the gym to cure it. To my misfortune, I suffered a muscle fibre rupture. I was bedridden for many months. Meanwhile, the coaching classes went on. I could not attend them or attend the IIT lectures.

When it was mandatory to be present at the IIT campus, I booked an Uber and laid down at the back seat. A one-way trip cost ₹350. Frequent visits to the IIT-D campus, getting MRIs done, appointments with the orthopaedist, and medicines depleted my savings.

I was back to square one. My dream of becoming a civil servant was ruined. If I had to pick it up again, it would have to be right from the beginning. Thankfully, I had been posting a lot about JEE on the internet while I was bedridden. There came a time in 2018 when hardly any IIT aspirant didn't know me. I caught the attention of a top management professional of one of India's leading banks. He came to Delhi to meet me and granted me angel funds.

Coincidentally, I had been thinking of starting my edtech venture. Back in 2018, there wasn't online learning for JEE. I launched it and, within no time, it flourished and generated huge profits. Many people started joining the platform as educators and learners. I was still an inexperienced 19-year-old, running my first venture. I worked day and night to make it grow.

However, I kept no secrets from an employee of mine. I thought telling him everything would empower him to work more efficiently, and keeping secrets was anyway immoral. When he started having difficulties in life, he started creating cock-and-bull stories to defame me. He used all the power, fame, funds and devices that I gave him against me. Getting backstabbed by your friend is not something one can withstand. It was my *et tu, Brute* moment. He projected me as a scammer. Many people were already intimidated and upset with my sudden growth. The libels quickly got viral. If you Googled my name in those days, it would show scammers as a suggestion on top. It was scary.

The education industry is all about reputation. In a matter of a few days, my life was overturned. Surplus funds became debts, fame turned into infamy, courage turned into paranoia, peaks turned into valleys. My hard work turned to dust. Again I was back to square one. This time I was diseased, depressed, defamed, debt-ridden and deserted. I was afraid to take on new endeavours. I was sceptical about people.

When funds left me, friends left me as well. Getting insulted became an everyday thing for me. As almost everyone insulted me, I even started to consider myself worthy of only insults. I got so consumed by depression that I failed six courses straight in a semester. I used to think that people who commit suicide are weak, but when I got such thoughts myself, I could empathise with them.

The defamation and estrangement went so far that my peers avoided taking me into their group project teams. I had to let go of the project marks in many courses, which led me to fail in many other courses. This gave rise to a series of F (fail) grades in my degree. I failed more than 20 courses during my college years. At all moments, I was clueless as to what would happen next. My world had fallen apart. I was afraid if I would even be placed. What was worse was, even if I reached the interview round, I was scared if the interviewer would ask me if I was that 'scammer'.

I was afraid that no one would do business with me because of my ruined reputation. However, my friend Dakshay, who had known me for five years, proposed to me his idea of a restaurant-chain venture. Above everything else, it seemed like the only feasible career option for me. I took more loans and carried out market research with him. Sadly, he was advised by four random people to be wary of me. Many of my juniors withheld other juniors from meeting me. I was alone in my corner room.

There came a time when I totally stopped speaking Hindi because I had no one who could talk to me in Hindi. I used to go to a gurudwara and do *kirtan*. All I had was the congregation that mostly spoke Punjabi. It helped me gain native fluency in Punjabi even though I had never lived in Punjab.

Eventually, the seventh semester of college began. I could not concentrate on my studies due to depression and anxiety. The exams were so rigorous that failure was inevitable without focused studying. The very thought of exams approaching made me restless. I mostly stayed alone or with Dakshay. The new venture was the only way to engage myself. I enjoyed the market research process a lot.

In March 2020, Covid-19 reached India, and the lockdown was imposed. At that point, no one knew how long the lockdown would go on. The pandemic happened just before my Minor 2 exams. Frankly, the announcement of the lockdown was a relief for me.

I thought of utilising that time to improve my English. I thought that the lockdown would at best go on for two weeks. But it went on and on and on and I learnt English on and on and on. I developed a vast vocabulary and learnt the powerful magic of words. I gained confidence and a good command of the language. The lockdown continued till December 2020. Colleges were not fully opened till December 19, 2021. In the meantime, I authored two books and tried to return to the education industry. I faced some hatred in the beginning but finally I got going. One of the books became a bestseller. It is now the most popular book for JEE strategy.

Meanwhile, academics at IIT-D were shifted online. Now I did courses with my juniors. Surprisingly, I did many courses with students who were inspired by my posts during their JEE. They paid me back by helping me in academics. Meanwhile, in January 2021, Dakshay and I launched our first outlet as soon as the lockdown was lifted. I was hopeful again and took a big loan for this new venture. We grew fast, but the Covid cases slowly started rising in our city. The markets were gradually deserted. Our fixed expenditure (rent, electricity bills, salaries, etc) was constant, but we had no crowd to generate sales. We suffered ₹90,000 in losses every month.

Then came another lockdown. It was a miserable period. We kept hearing about the deaths of people we knew, sometimes even our relatives. We could not let our employees' families starve; so we paid them salaries even during the lockdown. Thus far, I had accumulated a debt of more than ₹20 lakh. At this point, I opted to exit from the restaurant venture. It was uncertain whether it was a temporary exit or permanent. I was indecisive.

During the second lockdown, I had to do something to get rid of the debt and complete my degree. My degree was already extended by a year. It was my 10th semester. Even a small shortcoming or failure could extend my degree by another year.

I could not afford to have that. I was on tenterhooks during that period. With no option left, I made another return to the education industry. This time I got a lucrative offer from India's largest online learning platform. Not that I had not got such offers in the past, but I had always refused them in order to focus on my ventures. This time I accepted the offer.

I did my work religiously and paid off all my debts within a few months. Now I had enough funds to afford psychological help. Dakshay continued to run the restaurant venture. Parallelly, I started gaining massive traction in the education domain once again. I got a proposal to be the co-founder of an edtech venture—from Devansh, one of my earlier followers, who had now reached the third year of his college.

I had received similar propositions in the past, but I had developed an aversion to edtech ventures due to bitter experiences. This time it was different. The thinking resonated with me, and we created 'Verse', a platform for teaching all courses at all levels, for all levels.

In November 2021, I got my IIT degree.

Fast-forward to December 2021:

1. Howdy is a profitable and rapidly growing restaurant chain.
2. Verse is funded.
3. I am free of debts and I have some stable sources of income.
4. My follower base has grown to 150k.

My story has not ended yet. I am just 22 and excited for the upcoming events of my life.

The body, sluggish, aged, cold—the embers left from earlier fires,

The light in the eye grew dim, shall duly flame again.

— Walt Whitman

IIT Kharagpur and the Confidence it Instilled in Me

Akanksha Swarnim

2007-2012, B. Arch - Architecture, S. N. Hall, IIT Kharagpur

Akanksha Swarnim's biggest takeaway from Kharagpur was the confidence it instilled in her—so that she could stand on her own legs and make a difference. She could observe and understand different types of challenges in different aspects of life around her. In Gurgaon, she came to know about Upay, a footpath pathshala concept.

From childhood, Akanksha had been a person with great empathy. Whenever she saw youngsters at the traffic lights, crossing the road with begging bowls in hand, she had an urge from within to help them. She felt secure financially and in all other ways, but she wanted to do more—something useful to society. Akanksha started searching on the internet about opportunities to do volunteer community work. Soon she came to know about Varun Srivastava, the founder of Upay, and learned that he was also from IIT Kharagpur.

My father passed away when I was just nine years old. My mother brought me up. When I was in Class 6, someone told me about IIT Kharagpur and said if I wanted to achieve something in life I should go there. After that, I had only one aim—getting into IIT.

I belong to Pusa in Bihar, a small university town. There were only two schools here. In every class, I used to study hard and stand first. My mother was confident that she could send me out for special training to enter IIT. I went to Resonance Institute in Kota. I studied for two years there and I qualified for IIT Kharagpur. I had an interest in arts from childhood and therefore I chose architecture.

In Kharagpur, I met students from all over India and my perspective broadened in a big way. I was from a very small place and being in Kharagpur and meeting students from all over India was a learning in itself for me on a personal level.

From Kharagpur, I got the opportunity to go to Hong Kong in my fourth year for an internship. It was the first time I was going abroad alone. As a girl from a very small place, it was a very big accomplishment for me and it made my mother very proud.

My biggest takeaway from Kharagpur was the confidence it instilled in me to be able to stand on my legs and make a difference. I was able to observe and understand different kinds of challenges in different aspects of life around me. I could also think of possible solutions and their implementation.

While in campus, I was offered an interesting job at Ericsson in Kolkata. Even though I was a single woman living in Kolkata, I felt quite confident, thanks to IIT Kharagpur.

At Ericsson, I was given a big responsibility and posted in Noida near Delhi. Ericsson was a very big company and the people there were very happy with me. However, I was interested in understanding the overall business process and wanted to work for a start-up. So, I joined Peppertap in Gurgaon as a business analyst. There I led the customer experience team from the very beginning. I hired staff and designed ways of working for them. I also helped the company optimise various level of operations.

Coming from a small place in Bihar, working in Gurgaon was an enriching experience for me. My major learning was the ability to have a positive outlook that enabled one to solve any problem with ease. I was working with a cross-functional team and I learned how to deal with people in an assertive way and get the job done. My work was highly appreciated by the company's management.

In Gurgaon I came to know about Upay, a footpath *pathshala* concept.

From childhood, I was a person with great empathy. Whenever I saw youngsters at traffic signals with begging bowls in hand, I had an urge to help them. I felt secure financially. But, in other ways, but I wanted to do more—something useful for society. I started searching on the internet for a platform to do volunteer community work. Then I came to know about Varun Srivastava and learned that he was also from IIT Kharagpur. He is the founder of Upay.

I told him that I wanted to volunteer for the noble work he was doing. He said that there was no centre in Gurgaon and I could start one there under his guidance. Varun told me to go to places where there were shanties (*jhopris*) and talk to the dwellers there. The purpose was to build a rapport with them and win their trust. My stint at IIT Kharagpur helped me in this, as this is where I had learnt the ability to connect with people. That was because, in Kharagpur, I had to connect with students from all over India. The social events in IIT Kharagpur helped me in a big way to make friends with anyone and everyone. This was something I wouldn't have got if I had remained in Bihar. Kharagpur gave me a very wide exposure to many things in life.

My next job was to get a couple of children from each *jhopri* to study. This was a big task as neither they nor their parents had ever been to a school.

My few friends (who had joined me) and I used to go to the *jhopri*, armed with a plastic mattress and a foldable board, and hold classes under a tree. My husband also joined me.

The main challenges were:

- how to mobilise volunteers to teach
- how to retain the volunteers, who were put off by the idea of going to a slum

These volunteers were also put off by the dirty conditions and the heat, as they were used to working in air-conditioned offices in Gurgaon for multinational companies.

Out of a hundred volunteers, we were able to retain only ten.

To increase our reach to get long-term volunteers, we used social media and visited parks where young and energetic people, as well as older people, came for a morning run.

Money was raised through fundraising initiatives. The team members explained to potential donors the kind of work we had taken up, the difficult teaching conditions we had to face, and our commitment to make a change. Initially, Varun provided some money to kickstart the initiative. After that, we collected money from friends and family.

Akanksha Swarnim taking a class

We found that children were not only intelligent but also highly motivated to learn. This gave us immense satisfaction. We could feel the change happening.

At the moment, we have four centres in Gurgaon and three in NCR. Each centre has about 50 to 60 children.

The IIT Kharagpur connection helped me at every level. If we went to IIT Kharagpur alumni for support, they believed in us and came forward in their own way to help. They also helped in connecting us with the right people to get land, funding, school supplies, etc. Corporate level fundraising become a reality at this stage as we were able to instil confidence, having worked at the ground level for a couple of years.

One of my colleagues, who deserves special mention in the noble work we are committed to, is Ms Harsha Rani, who is also from Bihar. She is a resident of S N Hall, from the chemical engineering department of IIT Kharagpur. She is the founder of Upay in Bengaluru and currently running two centres there. As a result of this work, we find our lives more meaningful.

Chapter 5

Notable IITians

There are some notable ones who give IIT its special brand name.

According to a study, over 75% of the CEOs of multinationals are IITians. This is a list of a few notable IITians, based on research on social media and the internet. However, this is not an exhaustive list in any way.

Sundar Pichai
CEO, Alphabet Inc

Pichai Sundararajan was born on June 10, 1972. Better known as Sundar Pichai, he is an Indian-born American business executive. He is the chief executive officer (CEO) of Alphabet Inc and its subsidiary Google.

Born in Madurai, India, Pichai earned his degree from **IIT Kharagpur** in metallurgical engineering. Moving to the United States, he attained an MS from Stanford University in materials science and engineering and then attained an MBA from the Wharton School of the University of Pennsylvania, where he was named a Siebel Scholar and a Palmer Scholar, respectively.

Pichai began his career as a materials engineer. Following a short stint at the management consulting firm McKinsey & Co., Pichai joined Google in 2004, where he led the product management and innovation efforts for a suite of Google's client software products, including Google Chrome and Chrome OS, as well as being largely responsible for Google Drive. In addition, he went on to oversee the development of other applications such as Gmail and Google Maps. In 2010, Pichai also announced the open-sourcing of the new video codec VP8 by Google and introduced the new video format, WebM. The Chromebook was released in 2012. In 2013, Pichai added Android to the list of Google products that he oversaw.

Pichai was selected to become the next CEO of Google on August 10, 2015, after previously being appointed Product Chief by CEO Larry Page. On October 24, 2015, he stepped into the new position at the completion of the formation of Alphabet Inc., the new holding company for the Google company family. He was appointed to the Alphabet Board of Directors in 2017.

Pichai was included in Time's annual list of the 100 most influential people in 2016 and 2020.

Parag Aggarwal
CEO, Twitter

Dr. Agrawal obtained his B. Tech. degree in computer science and engineering from **IIT Bombay** in 2005 and a PhD in computer science from Stanford University in 2011.

Prior to joining Twitter, Dr. Agrawal did research in large-scale data management with collaborators at Microsoft Research, Yahoo! Research and AT and T Labs. He started his journey with Twitter in 2011 as a distinguished software engineer and led efforts to scale Twitter Ad systems, as well as re-accelerating user growth by improving home timeline relevance. He became the chief technical officer in 2017 and was responsible for Twitter's technical strategy and for overseeing machine learning and AI across the company. On November 29, 2021, Dr. Agrawal was appointed as the new CEO of Twitter and is responsible for overseeing all operations at the major global tech company.

Arvind Krishna
CEO, IBM

Arvind Krishna is an Indian-American business executive serving as the chairman and CEO of IBM. He has been the CEO of IBM since April 2020 and took on the role of chairman in January 2021. Krishna began his career at IBM in 1990, at the Thomas J. Watson Research Center, and was promoted to senior vice-president in 2015, managing IBM Cloud and Cognitive Software and IBM Research divisions. He was a principal architect of the acquisition of Red Hat, the largest acquisition in the company's history.

He received a B. Tech degree in electrical engineering from **IIT Kanpur** in 1985. He subsequently moved to the United States to earn a PhD in electrical engineering from the University of Illinois at Urbana-Champaign in 1991. He is the recipient of distinguished alumni awards from both IIT Kanpur and the University of Illinois Urbana-Champaign.

Arvind Krishna led the building and expansion of new markets for IBM in artificial intelligence, cloud, quantum computing and blockchain. He was a driving force behind IBMs $34-billion acquisition of Red Hat, which closed in July 2019. In 2021, he was named by CRN as the year's 'Most Influential Executive'.

Arun Sarin
Former CEO, Vodafone Plc

Arun Sarin was formerly the CEO of InfoSpace, CEO of Vodafone for Asia/Pacific region, and president and COO of Airtouch Communications. Sarin serves on the boards of Directors of Vodafone Plc, Charles Schwab Corp, Cisco Systems, Gap Inc, and Accel-KKR. He is also a director of several non-profit and educational organisations and is a graduate of **IIT Kharagpur**.

Victor Menezes
Former Senior Vice-Chairman, Citigroup

Victor was responsible for Citigroup's businesses in the Emerging Markets and covers all of its activities across its corporate and consumer franchises in 80 countries. He also had the global product responsibility for e-business and worldwide securities services. He has served at Citibank in various positions and in various continents since 1972. He is a graduate of **IIT Bombay**.

Prith Banerjee
CTO, Ansys; former CTO of ABB and Schneider Electric

During the 35 years after PhD, Prith Banerjee believes that he has been fortunate to have received broad experience around research and development, with 15 years of experience in several Fortune 100 companies (HP, ABB, Schneider Electric, Accenture and Ansys), experience in two start-up companies

(Accelchip and Binachip), and 22 years of experience in academia, in both public and private universities (University of Illinois and Northwestern). He is a graduate of **IIT Kharagpur**.

Kanwal Rekhi
CEO, Ensim; Founder, TIE

Kanwal Rekhi has over 20 years of executive experience at successful Silicon Valley technology companies. Kanwal was one of the original founders of Excelan, a computer networking company founded in 1982, where he was named president and CEO in 1985. Excelan merged with Novell in 1989, and Rekhi remained at Novell as an EVP and CTO. He is currently the chairman of the board of trustees for The Indus Entrepreneurs association (TIE). Kanwal attended **IIT Bombay** and earned an MS in electrical engineering from Michigan Technological University, which honoured him with a PhD in business and engineering in 1997.

Manoj Singh
CEO, Deloitte Consulting, Asia/Pacific

Manoj Singh joined the firm in 1979 and became partner in 1986. He has been a partner in the firm since 1986. Previously he served as Deloitte Consulting's managing director for the Americas. Singh is also a member of the board of directors for Deloitte Consulting and is a graduate of **IIT Kanpur**.

Vinod Khosla
Founder, Sun Microsystems; General Partner, Kleiner Perkins Caufield and Byers

Vinod Khosla was co-founder of Daisy Systems and founding chief executive officer of Sun Microsystems, where he pioneered open systems and commercial RISC processors. He serves on the boards of Asera, Centrata, Indian School of Business, Infinera, Juniper Networks, Kovio, OnFiber Communications, QWEST Communications, Zambeel and Zaplet. Khosla has a  master's in biomedical engineering from Carnegie Mellon University and an MBA from Stanford Graduate School of Business. He is a graduate of **IIT Delhi.**

Mohan Sawhney
McCormick Tribune Professor of Technology and Director, Center for Research in Technology and Innovation, Kellogg School of Management

Prof Mohan Sawhney is a globally recognised scholar and speaker in technology marketing and e-business strategy. He has pioneered concepts like business-to-business hubs, metamarkets, synchronisation, community-centric innovation and collaborative marketing. *Business Week* named him one of the 25 most influential  people in e-business. He has received several awards for teaching and research, including the Outstanding Professor of the Year award at Kellogg. He advises large technology companies, governments and start-up technology companies worldwide. He is a fellow of the World Economic Forum. He is a graduate of **IIT Delhi.**

Gursharan S. Sidhu
Founder, I2 technologies

Gursharan Sidhu was founder, board member, CTO, senior VP of engineering at ipVerse.

Sidhu, was, over a period of 15 years, senior director, Network Systems Development, and then Apple Fellow at Apple Computer. Before that, he was the advisor to the Government of Mexico and a senior  professor at Universidad Nacional Autonoma de Mexico and held faculty positions at SUNY Buffalo and Stanford University. He is a member of the board of trustees of the Smithsonian Institution's Freer and Sackler Galleries and president of the board of SACHI. He is a graduate of **IIT Madras.**

Narayan Murthy
Founder, Infosys

Nagavara Ramarao Narayana Murthy (born 20 August 1946) is an Indian billionaire businessman. He is the founder of Infosys and was the chairman, chief executive officer (CEO), president, and chief  mentor of the company before retiring and taking the title 'chairman emeritus'. As of October 2021, his net worth was estimated at US$4.3 billion.

Murthy was born and raised in Shidlaghatta, Karnataka. He has a master's degree from the **IIT Kanpur.**

Before starting Infosys, Murthy worked at the Indian Institute of Management Ahmedabad as the chief systems programmer and Patni Computer Systems in Pune (Maharashtra). He started Infosys in 1981 and was the CEO from 1981 to 2002 as well as the chairman from 2002 to 2011. In 2011, he stepped down from the board and became the chairman emeritus. In June 2013, Murthy was appointed as the executive chairman for a period of five years.

Murthy has been listed among the 12 greatest entrepreneurs of our time by *Fortune* magazine. He has been described as the 'Father of the Indian IT Sector' by *Time* magazine and CNBC for his contribution to outsourcing in India. Murthy has been honoured with the Padma Vibhushan and Padma Shri awards.

Gururaj 'Desh' Deshpande
Founder and Chairman, Sycamore Networks Inc

Prior to co-founding Sycamore Networks, Desh was the founder and chairman of Cascade Communications Corp. Before Cascade, he co-founded Coral Network Corporation in 1988. His generous donations have made possible MIT's Deshpande Center for Technological Innovation. He has an ME in electrical engineering from the University of New Brunswick in Canada and a PhD in data communications from Queens University in Canada. He is a graduate of **IIT Madras**.

Dr. Suhas Patil
Founder, Cirrus Logic

Dr. Patil is founder of Cirrus Logic Inc, founded in 1981. Previously, he was an associate professor of computer science at the University of Utah and an assistant professor of electrical engineering at MIT. He has an honorary doctor of science degree from Indian Institute of Technology in 1995. He is also on the board of Cirrus Logic, RightWorks and Aspirian Inc. He is a graduate of **IIT Kharagpur**.

Pradeep Sindhu
Founder, Juniper Networks

Pradeep Sindhu founded Juniper Networks in 1996 and played a central role in the architecture, design and development of the M40 while running the company. He is now responsible for the company's technical roadmap and also plays an active role in the day-to-day design and development of future products. While at the Computer Science Lab at  Xerox PARC, Dr. Sindhu worked on design tools for VLSI and high-speed interconnects for shared-memory multiprocessors. This work led to the commercial development of Sun Microsystems' first high-performance multiprocessor system family. Dr. Sindhu holds a PhD in computer science from Carnegie Mellon University and a bachelor's degree in electrical engineering from **IIT Kanpur**.

Avi Nash
Advisory Director, Goldman Sachs

Avi Nash has been an advisory director of Goldman Sachs, after retiring as a partner in 2002. In this role, he is involved with several strategic, thematic and mentoring programmes for the firm. Avi joined the firm in 1987, became vice president in 1989, managing director in 1996, and a partner of Goldman  Sachs in 1998. Avi received a master of management degree with distinction from Northwestern University's Kellogg School in 1981. He has an MS (ChE) from Syracuse University (1977) and a B. Tech from **IIT Bombay** (1975).

Late Umang Gupta
Founder, Gupta Corporation

Umang Gupta is well-known as an early Silicon Valley entrepreneur. Gupta wrote the first business plan for Oracle in 1981. He was the founder and CEO of Gupta Corporation, the first Indian founded public software company in the USA. He and his wife Ruth took the lead in the founding of a Silicon Valley respite care home for developmentally disabled children, named Raji House, in memory of their son. In 2000, Gupta was the honoured recipient of the Asian Pacific Foundation Award for Civic Leadership and Philanthropy. He also serves on the board of the Peninsula Community Foundation. He received his B. Tech from **IIT Kanpur** and his MBA from Kent State University.

Brijendra Syngal

Brijendra Syngal is a pioneer in the Indian telecommunication sector, and has been referred to as the 'Father of Internet and Data Services in India'. He headed the stunningly ambitious effort to make India the first country in the developing world to launch its own satellite-based communication connectivity across oceans and the inaccessible hilly terrains of Leh, Ladakh, Spiti, Andaman and Nicobar. He is a graduate of **IIT Kharagpur**.

Prof Prem Vrat

Prof Prem Vrat was the first director when IIT Roorkee was made an IIT. He facilitated the change. He was also the officiating director of IIT-D and is now pro-chancellor at NorthCap University, Gurugram. He is a graduate of IIT Kharagpur.

Davender Jain
Former UN advisor in Ghana; former Chief Monitoring coordinator of World Bank-aided projects; former Adviser with Parliament of NSW Sydney Australia

Davender Jain is the recipient of the RAREcitation of Columbia University N.Y, USA, for being an outstanding graduate student and a fellow of Columbia University. He was an advisor to the Parliament of NSW and the founder president of Ezesolutions Pty Ltd. He is a graduate of IIT Kharagpur.

Dr. Ravinder Nath Khanna
Founder and Chairman, CandS Electric Ltd

Dr. Ravinder Nath Khanna is a gold medallist and the recipient of the distinguished alumni award. He has a doctorate in entrepreneurship from KEISIE South Korea. He is a graduate of **IIT Kharagpur**.

Rameshwar K. Maini
CEO, Zentech

IIT Bombay not only gave Rameshwar Maini education, confidence and social connections to create the best foundation for a successful future, but it also provided every brick to build his company Zentech Inc.

Recently Zentech, in partnership with Blue Whale Ocean Filtration, developed vessels that are specifically designed for removal of microplastics from lakes and rivers.

Ajit Jain (born 1951) is an Indian-American executive who is the vice chairman of insurance operations at Berkshire Hathaway. He was raised in India's coastal state of Odisha. He did his schooling at Stewart School, Cuttack. In 1972, Jain graduated from **IIT Kharagpur** in India with a B. Tech degree in mechanical engineering.

From 1973 to 1976, Jain worked for IBM as a salesman for their data processing operations in India. He was named 'Rookie of the Year' in his region in 1973. He lost his job in 1976 when IBM discontinued its operation in India because it declined to allow any Indian ownership of the company, as was then required by law. In 1978, Jain moved to the United States, where he earned an MBA from Harvard University and joined McKinsey & Co. He returned to India in the early 1980s and got married. The Jains then moved back to the United States, as Jain's wife preferred to live there.

In 1986, he left McKinsey to work on insurance operations for Warren Buffett. Jain was invited by his former boss, Michael Goldberg, who had left McKinsey & Co to join Berkshire Hathaway in 1982. At the time, he said he knew little about the insurance business.

In the annual letter to shareholders on 2014, it was suggested that both Jain and Greg Abel could be appropriate successors to Warren Buffett as CEO of Berkshire Hathaway. In January 2018, Jain was named Berkshire Hathaway's vice chair of insurance operations and appointed to Hathaway's board of directors. Jain lives in the New York City area.

Sushanta Kumar Bhattacharyya, Baron Bhattacharyya (6 June 1940 – 1 March 2019) was a British-Indian engineer, educator and government advisor. In 1980, he became a professor of manufacturing systems at the University of Warwick and founded the Warwick Manufacturing Group. In 2004 he was made a Life Peer and became a member of the House of Lords.

Kumar Bhattacharyya was born in Bangalore, as the elder son of Sudhir Kumar Bhattacharyya and Hemanalini Chakraborty. Of Bengali origin, the Bhattacharyyas were a *zamindari* family from Dhaka District (then in the Bengal Presidency of British India and now in Bangladesh). At the time, his father was a professor at the Indian Institute of Science in Bangalore, where Bhattacharyya spent the first 12 years of his life. Bhattacharyya's father was a distinguished professor of physical chemistry and subsequently a fellow of the Indian National Science Academy.

In 1952, upon his father's appointment as head of the chemistry department at the new Indian Institute of Technology, Kharagpur, the family moved to Kharagpur.

Bhattacharyya studied mechanical engineering at **IIT Kharagpur**. The following year, he moved to Britain, where he worked for six years as a graduate apprentice at Lucas Industries, a large British manufacturing company.

Lord Bhattacharyya's contribution to innovation in academia and industry led to several prime ministerial visits to WMG. Margaret Thatcher called Bhattacharyya "a true pioneer" in a 1990 speech opening WMG's Advanced Technology Centre. A decade later, the Labour Prime Minister, Tony Blair, said WMG was "an outstanding example of combining academic excellence with industrial relevance." In a 2007 speech, Blair's successor, Gordon Brown, said that WMG "provides a prime example of how the knowledge created in our universities can be transferred to make a difference in the real world."

Bhattacharyya was appointed a Commander of the Order of the British Empire (CBE) in the 1997 New Year Honours and knighted in 2003. On 3 June 2004, he was made a life peer as 'Baron Bhattacharyya' of Moseley in the County of West Midlands. He sat on the Labour benches in the House of Lords.

In 2014, he was elected a Fellow of the Royal Society (FRS).

Some others who deserve a mention

- Srikumar Banerjee, Former Director, Bhabha Atomic Research Centre
- Mani Lal Bhaumik, Indian-born American physicist

- Rono Dutta, CEO, IndiGo airlines and Former CEO, United Airlines
- Vinod Gupta, Founder and Former Chairman and CEO, Infogroup, USA
- Raj Kamal Jha, Chief Editor, The Indian Express, and writer
- Pradeep K. Khosla, 8th Chancellor of University of California, San Diego
- S. Rao Kosaraju, who developed Kosaraju's algorithm, which finds the strongly connected components of a directed graph
- Arunabh Kumar, CEO and Co-founder, The Viral Fever
- Jitendra Kumar, Co-founder, The Viral Fever
- Narendra Kumar, Physicist, Padmashree recipient
- Sankar Kumar Nath, Geophysicist, Shanti Swarup Bhatnagar Laureate
- Janardan Ganpatrao Negi, Theoretical Geophysicist, Shanti Swarup Bhatnagar Laureate
- Surendra Prasad, Communications Engineer, Shanti Swarup Bhatnagar Laureate
- Basanta Kumar Sahu, Mathematical Geologist, Shanti Swarup Bhatnagar Laureate
- Biswapati Sarkar, Co-founder, The Viral Fever
- Duvvuri Subbarao, 22nd Governor, Reserve Bank of India

Chapter 6

All About the Newer IITs

(Source: Wikipedia)

IIT Guwahati

Indian Institute of Technology Guwahati (IIT Guwahati) is a public technical university established by the Government of India, located in Guwahati, in the state of Assam in India. It is the sixth Indian Institute of Technology established in India. IIT Guwahati is officially recognised as an Institute of National Importance by the Government of India. IIT Guwahati has been ranked 7th in engineering and 8th in the overall category in NIRF India Rankings 2021.

The history of IIT Guwahati traces its roots to the 1985 Assam Accord signed between the All Assam Students Union and the Government of India, which mentions the general improvement in education facilities in Assam and specifically the setting up of an IIT.

IIT Guwahati was established in 1994 by an Act of Parliament and its academic programme commenced in 1995. IIT Guwahati admitted its first batch of students into its bachelor of technology programme in 1995. The selection process was the same as that of the other IITs, i.e., through the Joint Entrance Examination. In 1998, the first batch of students were accepted into the master of technology programme through GATE.

The campus of IIT Guwahati is on the northern banks of Brahmaputra and abuts the North Guwahati town of Amingaon. It is often considered the most beautiful campus in India. The campus is on a 700-acre plot of land, around 20 km from the heart of the city. It has the Brahmaputra on one side and hills and vast open spaces on other sides.

IIT Guwahati is a fully residential campus. All the students live in hostels on the campus. The hostels are named after rivers and tributaries of Northeast India: Manas, Dihing, Kapili, Siang, Kameng, Barak, Subansiri (girls' hostel), Umiam, Dibang, Brahmaputra (largest hostel in all the IITs), Dhansiri (new girls' hostel), Lohit and Disang (new boys' hostel). Apart from these, there is a married scholars' hostel for married postgraduates. Every student at IIT Guwahati is given a separate room. Each room comes equipped with the requisite basic amenities. The toilets and bathrooms are shared (three of each for every ten rooms on average). Every hostel has a mess, a canteen, a juice centre, a stationery shop, a library, a TV room, a sports room (for indoor sports), and laundry facilities. The hostels are provided with 24-hour internet facility. The boys' hostels are single seated, i.e., every boarder gets a single room.

Departments

- Department of Biosciences and Bioengineering
- Department of Chemical Engineering
- Center of Excellence for Sustainable Polymers
- Department of Chemistry
- Department of Civil Engineering
- Department of Computer Science and Engineering
- Department of Design
- Department of Electronics and Electrical Engineering (previously known as the Department of Electronics and Communication)
- Department of Humanities and Social Sciences
- Department of Mathematics
- Department of Mechanical Engineering
- Department of Physics

IIT Roorkee

Indian Institute of Technology Roorkee (IIT Roorkee) is a public technical university located in Roorkee, Haridwar district, Uttarakhand, India, headed by Director Ajit Kumar Chaturvedi. It was formerly known as University of Roorkee (1949–2001) and Thomason College of Civil Engineering (1847–1949). Established in 1847 in British India by the then lieutenant governor, Sir James Thomason, it is the oldest technical institution in Asia. It was given university status in 1949 and was converted into an Indian Institute of Technology in 2001, thus becoming the seventh IIT. IIT Roorkee has 22 academic departments covering engineering, applied sciences, humanities and social sciences, and management programmes with a strong emphasis on scientific and technological education and research.

The institution has its origins in a class started in 1845 to train local youth in engineering to assist in public works then beginning. In 1847 it was officially established. It was renamed Thomason College of Civil Engineering in 1854 in honour of its founder, James Thomason, lieutenant governor (1843–53). The first Indian to graduate from the Roorkee College was Rai Bahadur Kanhaiya Lal in 1852.

The Department of Civil Engineering was established in 1847 and it is the oldest engineering department in India. The electrical engineering department of the Thomson College was established in the year 1897, and it was one of the earliest such specialisations in the world. The architecture department is the first in India in instituting a master's degree course in architecture (M. Arch) in the year 1969–70.

In 1978, the Institute of Paper Technology, Saharanpur was merged with the then University of Roorkee. The Institute of Paper Technology was established as the School of Paper Technology by the Government of India in 1964, with aid from the Royal Swedish

Government. The school was renamed the Institute of Paper Technology in July 1968 and subsequently the Department of Paper Technology in July 1992.

The first edition of Thomso, the institute's annual cultural festival, was held in 1982.

On 21st September 2001, an ordinance issued by the Government of India declared it the nation's seventh Indian Institute of Technology, renaming it to the current name, Indian Institute of Technology Roorkee. The ordinance was converted into an act by the Parliament to make IIT Roorkee an Institution of National Importance.

The main campus in Roorkee has an area of 365 acres (1,480,000 m).

IIT Roorkee has a separate campus of 25 acres (100,000 m) in Saharanpur, which offers courses in polymer science, process engineering, paper technology, and packaging technology. In addition to this, a new ten-acre campus has been established in Greater Noida, Knowledge Park II, which was inaugurated on 4th April 2011. The Noida extension centre has 16 lecture rooms, software laboratories, faculty offices, a library and a computer centre.

Departments

- Engineering and Applied Sciences
  - Architecture and Planning
  - Applied Science and Engineering
  - Biotechnology
  - Chemical Engineering
  - Chemistry
  - Civil Engineering
  - Computer Science and Engineering
  - Earthquake Engineering
  - Earth Sciences
  - Electrical Engineering

- Electronics and Communication Engineering
- Humanities and Social Sciences
- Hydrology
- Hydro and Renewable Energy
- Management Studies
- Mathematics
- Mechanical and Industrial Engineering
- Metallurgical and Materials Engineering
- Paper Technology
- Polymer and Process Engineering
- Physics
- Water Resources Development and Management
- Sciences
  - Chemistry
  - Mathematics
- Business
  - Management Studies
- Humanities
  - Humanities and Social Sciences

IIT Ropar

Indian Institute of Technology Ropar (IIT Ropar) is a public technical university located in Rupnagar, Punjab, India. It is one of the eight newer Indian Institutes of Technology established by the Ministry of Human Resource Development (MHRD), Government of India under the Institutes of Technology (Amendment) Act, 2011 to expand the reach and enhance the quality of technical education in the country.

IIT Ropar was established by MHRD in 2008. The classes for academic session 2008–2009 were held at IIT Delhi. The institute started functioning from its transit campus in Rupnagar in August 2009.

IIT Ropar has completely shifted to its permanent campus since June 2019. Campus architecture is inspired by Indus Valley Civilisation with four 41-feet-high stone carved pillars at the entrance. The institute started to operate from its permanent campus from July 2018. Some phases of this campus were still under construction. The campus was being built on the land earlier known as Birla Seed Farms. It is located over an area of 525 acres (2.12 km). The foundation stone for the permanent campus was laid on 24th February 2009 by the Union HRD Minister Arjun Singh. The contract was given to CPWD and a Bangkok-based construction company was assigned the task of finishing the first phase. The computer science department has been shifted to this campus in July 2018. A part of the administration office was shifted on 17 June 2018. In June 2019, the administration and the departments of electrical, computer science and mechanical engineering completely shifted to the permanent campus.

The institute currently has 11 departments, 1 multi-disciplinary centre and 1 DST Technology Innovation Hub.

Departments

- Chemical Engineering
- Chemistry
- Civil Engineering
- Computer Science and Engineering
- Electrical Engineering
- Humanities and Social Sciences
- Mathematics and Computing
- Metallurgical and Materials Engineering
- Mathematics
- Mechanical Engineering
- Physics
- Center for Biomedical Engineering

IIT Bhubaneswar

Indian Institute of Technology Bhubaneswar (IIT Bhubaneswar) is a public technical university established by the Government of India in 2008, located in Bhubaneswar, Odisha, India.

The institute admits students for bachelor's and master's programmes via JEE Advanced and Graduate Aptitude Test in engineering respectively. The permanent campus at Argul, Khordha District was inaugurated by the current Prime Minister of India, Narendra Modi, on 24th December 2018. The areas of research are science, engineering and humanities.

Establishing an IIT in Odisha was a long-standing demand for several decades. As the state ranked at the bottom in terms of centrally funded academic and research institutions, there were strong allegations of Congress-led central government neglect. There were several incidents of protest, both locally in Odisha, the National Students Union of India (NSUI) and eminent non-resident Indian academics. An organisation called Agamee Odisha was formed and it spearheaded mass agitation throughout the state. There also have been stray incidents of violence related to the issue of Odisha's neglect. Politicians including the Chief Minister of Odisha, Naveen Patnaik, cast this festering issue as a sign of severe neglect of the state by the UPA government in New Delhi. In May 2007, this became a major issue in the Indian Parliament. The opposition NDA staged a walk-out in the Indian Parliament, accusing the ruling UPA of neglecting the state's economic development. Sections of the media reported that the Congress party-led UPA government had been embarrassed by this issue. Eventually, the HRD Minister, Arjun Singh, relented, leading to the inception of IIT Bhubaneswar.

The birth of the Indian Institute of Technology Bhubaneswar, came on the 60th anniversary of the country's Independence Day on 15th August 2007, when Dr Manmohan Singh, Prime Minister of India at that time, made the announcement about the expansion of the IIT system in the country. Further, the National Development Council of the Planning Commission, in its 54th meeting held on 19 December 2007, approved the proposal as part of the approval process of the 11th Five Year Plan (2007–12).

The Government of Odisha has allotted about 936 acres of government land for a permanent campus of the institute. In addition, the state government is acquiring about 16 acres of private land at its own cost to make the land contiguous. The foundation stone of the permanent campus at Arugul, on the outskirts of Bhubaneswar, was laid on 12th February 2009. Construction of a four-lane access road from National Highway 5 and provision of water and electric supply to the campus by the state government have made considerable progress. The Government of Odisha has also agreed to provide 75 acres of land along the Puri-Konark coastline to set up an Innovation Centre for Climate Change.

Departments

- Physics
- Chemistry
- Bio Science
- Mathematics
- Economics
- Electrical Engineering
- Metallurgy
- Material Engineering
- Geology
- Atmospheric
- Ocean Science
- English
- Psychology
- Mechanical Engineering
- Civil Engineering

- CSE
- ECE

IIT Gandhinagar

Indian Institute of Technology Gandhinagar (also known as IIT Gandhinagar or IITGN) is a public technical university located in Gandhinagar, Gujarat, India. It has been declared an Institute of National Importance by the Government of India. Established in 2008, the IIT Gandhinagar campus is spread over 400 acres of land along River Sabarmati. IIT Gandhinagar is one of the eight Indian Institutes of Technology (IITs) announced by the Ministry of Human Resource Development in 2008. The institute began operating in a temporary campus at Vishwakarma Government Engineering College, Chandkheda, mentored by Indian Institute of Technology Bombay. The first batch of students was admitted to three programmes: chemical engineering, mechanical engineering and electrical engineering.

IITGN was included in the Institutes of Technology (Amendment) Act, 2011. The Act was passed in the Lok Sabha on 24 March 2011 and by the Rajya Sabha on 30 April 2012.

The IIT Gandhinagar campus is located on the banks of the Sabarmati River in Palaj village. In 2011, in his inaugural speech at the Amalthea technology summit, the then Gujarat Chief Minister Narendra Modi spoke of the land for the new permanent campus, saying, "The state government has decided to give land on a 99-year-lease with a token amount of just one rupee for setting up a campus of IIT Gandhinagar." The institute took possession of over 400 acres of land in August 2012, and classes and other activities on the new campus began in July 2015.

Departments

- Biological Engineering
- Civil Engineering

- Chemical Engineering
- Computer Science and Engineering
- Electrical Engineering
- Mechanical Engineering
- Materials Engineering
- Chemistry
- Mathematics
- Physics
- Cognitive Science
- Earth Sciences
- Humanities and Social Sciences

IIT Hyderabad

Indian Institute of Technology Hyderabad (abbreviated IIT Hyderabad or IIT-H) is a public technical university located in Sangareddy district, Telangana, India.

IIT-H was founded in 2008; it is among the eight young Indian Institutes of Technology. It has 1,155 undergraduate, 635 master's and 1085 PhD students with 222 full-time faculty members.

IIT Hyderabad was established by the Ministry of Human Resource Development, Government of India under the Institutes of Technology (Amendment) Act, 2011. The Act was passed in the Lok Sabha on 24 March 2011 and by the Rajya Sabha on 30 April 2012. It was set up in technical and financial assistance from Government of Japan.

IIT Hyderabad began functioning on 18th August 2008 from a temporary campus in Ordnance Factory Medak, with Prof. U. B. Desai as the founding director. In July 2015, it moved to its 576-acre permanent campus at Kandi, Sangareddy. It is close to the outer ring road and located on NH-65.

The IIT-H campus is on a land area of 576 acres (234 hectares). The campus is designed by Pune-based acclaimed American architect, Prof. Christopher Charles Benninger. This organic campus is divided into clusters of buildings being completed in phases starting in 2011. The campus is one of India's best examples of energy efficient, carbon neutral and sustainable architecture. The design grew out of local weather conditions and utmost care to enhance learning. The graduate and postgraduate programmes are separated, student and teacher housing is divided, and girls' and boys' hostels are segregated for a pluralistic environment.

The 25 lakh square feet of buildings in Phase 1A, 3 academic blocks and 10 functioning hostel buildings (each with a capacity of 200) were completed in March 2019.

IIT Hyderabad has 18 engineering and science departments.

Departments

- Artificial Intelligence
- Biomedical Engineering
- Biotechnology
- Chemical Engineering
- Chemistry
- Climate Change
- Civil Engineering
- Computer Science and Engineering
- Design
- Electrical Engineering
- Engineering Science
- Entrepreneurship and Management
- Liberal Arts
- Materials Science and Metallurgical Engineering
- Mathematics
- Mechanical and Aerospace Engineering
- Physics
- Computational Engineering

IIT Jodhpur

Indian Institute of Technology Jodhpur (IIT Jodhpur or IIT-J) is a public technical university located in Jodhpur in the state of Rajasthan in India. It is one of the eight new Indian Institutes of Technology (IITs) established by the Ministry of Human Resource Development, Government of India under The Institutes of Technology (Amendment) Act, 2011 which declares these eight IITs as well as the conversion of the Institute of Technology, Banaras Hindu University to IIT. The Act was passed in the Lok Sabha on 24 March 2011 and by the Rajya Sabha on 30 April 2012.

IIT Jodhpur was first announced by the central government in July 2007, although the formal announcement was made in 2008, with IIT Kanpur mentoring IIT Jodhpur. In July 2008, the first academic session of IIT Jodhpur began at the IIT Kanpur campus, with 109 undergraduate students in computer science engineering, mechanical engineering and electrical engineering. The institute was sanctioned as an IIT for Rajasthan and not for Jodhpur in specific. It was after considering various cities, including Ajmer, Bikaner, Jaipur, Jodhpur, Kota and Udaipur, that the committee led by Prof Vijay Shankar Vyas suggested Jodhpur as the location for the IIT in Rajasthan. In late 2009, the MHRD granted final approval for establishing the institute at Jodhpur.

A portion of the MBM Engineering College under JNV University, Jodhpur was identified as the location for the transit campus of IIT Jodhpur. In May 2010, classes of IIT Jodhpur were shifted from IIT Kanpur to the transit campus in Jodhpur. In July 2017, the academic and residential campuses of IIT Jodhpur were migrated to the permanent campus. Construction of the permanent campus is still in progress.

IIT-J is located about 24 km from Jodhpur city on National Highway 62 which connects Jodhpur to Nagaur. The site spans over 852 acres (3.45 km) of land around Jhipasni and Gharao villages. M. M. Pallam

Raju, the then Union Minister for Human Resources Development, laid the foundation stone on 16th April 2013.

The permanent campus is being built on a self-sustainable model, catering for its own energy and water requirements. The masterplan of the campus got a GRIHA Exemplary Performance Award under the Passive Architecture Design category at the 8th GRIHA Summit held during 2–3 March 2017, at India Habitat Centre, New Delhi.

The institute has organised its academic activities to be conducted through 13 departments and schools.

Departments

- School of Artificial intelligence and Data science
- School of Management and Entrepreneurship
- Biosciences and Bioengineering
- Chemical Engineering
- Chemistry
- Civil Engineering
- Computer Science and Engineering
- Electrical Engineering
- Humanities and Social Sciences
- Metallurgical and Materials Engineering
- Mathematics
- Mechanical Engineering
- Physics

IIT Patna

Indian Institute of Technology Patna (IIT Patna or IIT-P) is a public technical university located in Patna, India. It is recognised as an Institute of National Importance by the Government of India. It is one of the new IITs established by an Act of the Indian Parliament on 6th August 2008.

The permanent campus of IIT Patna is located at Bihta, which is approximately 30 km from Patna, and has been fully operational since 2015.

IIT Patna's campus is located at Amhara, Bihta, 35 km from Patna at a 501-acre (203 ha) site. The foundation stone of the IIT Patna, Bihta Campus was laid by Kapil Sibal in 2011. IIT Patna started its new session (from July 2015) at its permanent campus located in Bihta. The campus in Bihta was inaugurated by Prime Minister Narendra Modi on 25th July 2015. Earlier, the institute was operating from a temporary 10-acre (4.0 ha) complex in Pataliputra colony, Patna, in buildings that have been renovated and were previously used by Naveen Government Polytechnic.

IIT Patna is the first IIT in the whole IIT system to start a M. Tech programme in nanotechnology. Admission to M. tech is through GATE after which an interview is held to screen the shortlisted candidates. Sponsored candidates are not required to appear in GATE and are directly called for interview on applying for admission to the M. Tech programme (if selected).

Started in 2009, PhD degrees are awarded by all the departments. Requirements for admission into the PhD programmes include a master's degree and prior academic achievement. Students undergo an interview before gaining admission.

Departments

- Chemical and Biochemical Engineering
- Civil and Environmental Engineering
- Computer Science and Engineering
- Electrical Engineering
- Mechanical Engineering
- Metallurgical and Materials Engineering
- Humanities and Social Sciences
- Endangered Language Studies

- Chemistry
- Physics
- Mathematics

IIT Indore

Indian Institute of Technology Indore (IIT Indore) is a public technical university located in Indore, Madhya Pradesh, India. IIT Indore was founded in 2009 and it is among the eight young Indian Institutes of Technology (IITs). IIT Indore is officially recognised as an Institute of National Importance by the Government of India.

Founded in 2009, it is one of the eight new Indian Institutes of Technology (IITs) established by the Ministry of Human Resource Development, Government of India under the Institutes of Technology (Amendment) Act, 2011 which declares eight new IITs as well as the conversion of Institute of Technology, Banaras Hindu University to IIT. The Act was passed in the Lok Sabha on 24 March 2011 and by the Rajya Sabha on 30 April 2012. Arjun Singh, the then HRD Minister of India, laid the foundation stone of IIT Indore on 17 February 2009 at its permanent campus located in Simrol, Indore, Madhya Pradesh. The institution started functioning from 2009 to 2010 in a temporary campus at Institute of Engineering and Technology of Devi Ahilya Vishwavidyalaya under the mentorship of IIT Bombay with Pradeep Mathur as the director. The first batch of IIT Indore graduated in 2013, and the institute celebrated its first Convocation Day on 8 June 2013.

IIT Indore is located at Simrol, Khandwa Road. The campus sprawls across 501.42 acres. IIT Indore moved from the two rented campuses to its permanent campus in Simrol in October 2015.

Departments

- Astronomy, Astrophysics and Space Engineering (AASE)
- Biosciences and Biomedical Engineering (BSBE)
- Chemistry

- Civil Engineering
- Computer Science and Engineering
- Electrical Engineering
- Humanities and Social Sciences
- Mathematics
- Mechanical Engineering
- Metallurgy Engineering and Materials Science
- Physics

IIT Mandi

Indian Institute of Technology Mandi (IIT Mandi) is a public technical and research university located in Mandi district of Himachal Pradesh.

Since the first batch of 97 students joined in July 2009, IIT Mandi has grown to currently host 125 faculty, 1,655 students (enrolled in various undergraduate, postgraduate and research programmes) and 1,141 alumni. Since the inception of the institute, IIT Mandi faculty have been involved in over 275 research and development projects worth more than Rs 120 crore. In the past 10 years, the institute has signed memorandum of understanding with as many as 11 international and 12 national universities.

IIT Mandi's permanent campus (about 14 km from Mandi) is fully functional on the left bank of the Uhl River at Kamand and Salgi villages in Mandi. Timothy A. Gonsalves is the founding Director (15/1/2010-30/6/2020) of IIT Mandi and R. C. Sawhney served as the first registrar. Prof Ajit Kumar Chaturvedi, Director, IIT Roorkee took charge as acting director from 1 July 2020.

IIT Mandi is one of eight Indian Institutes of Technology (IITs) established by the Ministry of Human Resource Development, Government of India in 2008 under the Institutes of Technology (Amendment) Act, 2011 which declares these eight IITs as well as the conversion of Institute of Technology, Banaras Hindu University to IIT. The Act was passed in the Lok Sabha on 24th March 2011 and by the Rajya Sabha on 30th April 2012. IIT Mandi was initially mentored by IIT Roorkee, which hosted the first batch of students.

The foundation stone was laid on 24th February 2009. IIT Mandi was registered as a society in Uttarakhand on 20 June 2009. Classes started in IIT Roorkee, the mentoring IIT, on 27th July 2009. The transit campus at Government Postgraduate College, Mandi was handed over by the Himachal Pradesh Government on 16th November 2009.

On 12 April 2012, the ground-breaking ceremony was held in the Kamand campus to mark the start of construction. On 25th April 2015, IIT Mandi became the first of all the new IITs to completely shift B. Tech. students to its permanent campus in Kamand.

Having started its journey in 2009 with 510 acres (210 ha) of grassland on the banks of River Uhlin the village Kamand of Himachal Pradesh, 460 kilometres (290 mi) away from New Delhi, the Indian Institute of Technology Mandi has made impressive and rapid strides towards creating a remarkable and unique campus in the challenging yet serene Himalayan set-up. The campus is split internally in two halves—the North Campus and the South Campus. Proper communication has been facilitated by the college for students, staff and faculty for communication between north and south campus.

Departments

- Civil Engineering
- Computer Science and Engineering
- Data Science and Engineering
- Electrical Engineering
- Engineering Physics
- Mechanical Engineering

IIT (BHU) Varanasi

Indian Institute of Technology (BHU) Varanasi (IIT BHU) is a public technical university located in Varanasi, Uttar Pradesh, India. Founded in 1919 as the Banaras Engineering College, it became the Institute of Technology, Banaras Hindu University in 1968. It was designated an Indian Institute of Technology in 2012. IIT (BHU) Varanasi has 16 departments, 3 inter-disciplinary schools and 1 humanities and social sciences section. It is located inside the Banaras Hindu University Campus.

IIT (BHU) Varanasi has formerly been known as Banaras Engineering College (BENCO), College of Mining and Metallurgy (MINMET), College of Technology (TECHNO) and Institute of Technology, Banaras Hindu University (IT-BHU). Its establishment is intimately linked with that of Banaras Hindu University (BHU). The first convocation ceremony at BHU was held on 2nd December 1920. The Chancellor of the University, Maharaja Krishnaraja Wadiyar of Mysore who had come to preside over and address the convocation, performed the opening ceremony of the Banaras Engineering College workshop buildings. An artisan course was started on 11th February 1919. BHU has the credit of first starting degree classes in mechanical engineering, electrical engineering, metallurgy and pharmaceutics, thanks to the foresight of its founder, Pt. Madan Mohan Malaviya.

Departments

- Architecture, Planning and Design
- Ceramic Engineering and Technology
- Chemical Engineering
- Civil Engineering
- Computer Science and Engineering
- Electrical Engineering
- Electronics and Communication Engineering
- Mechanical Engineering

- Metallurgical Engineering
- Mining Engineering
- Pharmaceutical Engineering and Technology

IIT Palakkad

Indian Institute of Technology Palakkad (IIT Palakkad or IIT PKD) is a public autonomous engineering and research institute located in Palakkad, Kerala. It is one of the five new IITs proposed in the 2014 Union Budget of India. The campus was inaugurated on 3rd August 2015 at the temporary campus site located inside the Ahalia Integrated Campus, Palakkad. In February 2019, academic activities commenced in the Nila campus in Kanjikode. The institute has 94 faculty, 978 students, and 63 non-teaching staff. IIT Palakkad was founded in 2015 with the Director of IIT Madras, Dr. Bhaskar Ramamurthi, as the mentor director. IIT Madras deputed a batch of experienced professors including the ones recently retired, former deans and heads of various departments to the new campus as both permanent and visiting professors. In January 2017, Dr. P. B. Sunil Kumar, who was the professor-in-charge, was appointed as the director by the President of India, Pranab Mukherjee.

IIT Palakkad currently functions in two campuses—the temporary campus and the Nila campus, which are separated by about 13 km. The temporary campus is at Ahalia Integrated campus in Kozhippara, Palakkad, which is about 20 km from Palakkad town. The temporary campus is 55,000 sq. ft. in area and consists of well-equipped academic classrooms, a seminar room, an auditorium, a conference room, a workshop, a library, a cafeteria, laboratories and faculty offices. It also provides hostel and sports and recreational facilities with access to high-speed internet. The Nila campus is set up in 30 acres out of the 504 acres allotted to the permanent campus site in Kanjikode. It houses two batches of undergraduate students. Facilities here include two boys' hostel and a girls' hostel, classrooms, a library and research labs. The construction of phase I permanent campus in a 500-acre plot at Kanjikode is ongoing.

IIT Palakkad has 8 departments.

Departments

- Civil Engineering
- Computer Science and Engineering
- Electrical Engineering
- Mechanical Engineering
- Chemistry
- Physics
- Mathematics
- Humanities

IIT Tirupati

Indian Institute of Technology Tirupati (IIT Tirupati) is an autonomous engineering and technology education institute located in Tirupati. It started functioning from 5th August 2015 in a temporary campus housed at Krishna Theja Educational Institutions in Chadalawada Nagar. Now, IIT Tirupati, the fastest growing third generation IIT, has a beautiful transit campus at Yerpedu and has shifted most of its operations from the temporary to the transit campus, which is a part of the 500+ acre permanent campus at the same site in Yerpedu.

Till 2016, a director was appointed by MHRD for IIT Tirupati. The Director of IIT Madras, Dr. Bhaskar Ramamurthi, was the mentor director. In 2017, Dr. K. N. Satyanarayana was appointed the director of IIT Tirupati.

IIT Tirupati was initially functioning from the campus of Chadalawada Group of Institutes in Tirupati, while the permanent building was coming up near Yerpedu, located between Renigunta and Srikalahasti. The hostel facility for boys and girls has been arranged at a transit campus (30 acres), Yerpedu, which is to come up as the permanent campus. The land acquisition (531 acres) for the permanent campus has been completed. The transit campus consists of a classroom complex, a computer lab, a library, a ground, a health centre, and engineering workshops for all trades. A few labs are still functioning from the temporary campus.

Departments

- Chemical Engineering
- Civil Engineering
- Computer Science and Engineering
- Electrical Engineering
- Mechanical Engineering

IIT (ISM) Dhanbad

Indian Institute of Technology (Indian School of Mines), Dhanbad (abbreviated IIT (ISM), Dhanbad) is a public technical university located in Dhanbad, India. It has a main campus of 218 acres in Sardar Patel Nagar area of Dhanbad, and recently the Jharkhand cabinet approved 226.98 acres of land in Nirsa for its second campus. The IIT (ISM) Dhanbad administration has plans to open more than 29 academic centres in this upcoming campus in Nirsa, Dhanbad. It is an Institute of National Importance. IIT (ISM) has 18 academic departments covering engineering, applied sciences, humanities and social sciences and management programmes. It was formerly known as Indian School of Mines, Dhanbad before its conversion into an Indian Institute of Technology (IIT).

IIT (ISM) Dhanbad is located in the mineral-rich region of India, in the city of Dhanbad. It is the third oldest institute (after IIT Roorkee and IIT (BHU) Varanasi), which got converted into an IIT. It was established by the British Indian Government on the lines of the Royal School of Mines – London. It was formally inaugurated on 9th December 1926 by Lord Irwin, the then Viceroy of India. It started as an institution to impart education in mining and mineral sciences, and today it has grown into a technical institution with various academic departments. IIT (ISM) Dhanbad admits its undergraduate students through Joint Entrance Examination (Advanced), previously IIT JEE.

The Indian National Congress at its XVII Session of December 1901 passed a resolution stating that: The Indian National Congress is of opinion that a Government College of Mining Engineering should be established in some suitable place in India on the models of the Royal School of Mines in England.

The McPherson Committee, formed by Government of British India, recommended the establishment of an institution for imparting education in the fields of mining and geology, whose report, submitted in 1920 along with the approach of Indian Mine Managers of India in 1924, formed the main basis for establishment of the Indian School of Mines and Applied Geology at Dhanbad on 9th December 1926. From 1926 to 1946 it was led by Prof F. W. Sharpley.

The institute originally offered courses mainly in mining engineering and applied geology when it opened. In 1957, the institute began offering courses in petroleum engineering and applied geophysics and the name was changed to Indian School of Mines.

Departments

- Chemical Engineering
- Civil Engineering
- Computer Science and Engineering
- Electrical Engineering
- Electronics Engineering
- Environmental Engineering

- Fuel, Mineral and Metallurgical Engineering
- Mechanical Engineering
- Mining Engineering
- Mining Machinery Engineering
- Petroleum Engineering
- Chemistry
- Applied Geology
- Applied Geophysics
- Mathematics and Computing
- Physics

IIT Bhilai

Indian Institute of Technology Bhilai (IIT Bhilai) is a public technical and research university located in Bhilai, Chhattisgarh, India. Classified as an Institute of National Importance, IIT-BH formally came into existence in July 2016 with the influx of the first batch of students on 25th July 2016. It is currently being mentored by IIT Hyderabad.

Until the infrastructure and permanent campus is ready, the institute will function temporarily at the campus of the Government Engineering College (GEC) Raipur. This temporary campus of IIT Bhilai is located in Sejbahar area on Old Dhamtari Road in Raipur. the four-storeyed Block B of the GEC building has been fully renovated and furnished for IIT Bhilai. The temporary campus is about 10 km from the main city of Raipur and is well-connected through public transport facilities to the railway station, airport and the city.

Presently, IIT Bhilai is functioning from its transit campus at GEC, Raipur. The transit campus of IIT Bhilai situated on Old Dhamtari Road in Raipur has been successfully operational since 2016. The four-storeyed Block B of GEC Raipur building has been furnished for academic activities at IIT Bhilai. Apart from this, IIT Bhilai has its own hostels for boys and girls provided by GEC Raipur in the campus. The transit campus is about 10 km from the main city of

Raipur and is well-connected through public transport to the railway station, airport and Raipur city.

Departments

- Electrical Engineering and Computer Science (includes CSE, EE and DSAI)
- Mechanical Engineering
- Physics
- Chemistry
- Mathematics
- Liberal Arts

IIT Dharwad

Indian Institute of Technology Dharwad (IIT Dharwad or IIT-DH) is an autonomous engineering and technology institute in Dharwad, Karnataka, India. IIT Dharwad started functioning from July 2016 in a temporary campus of the Water and Land Management Institute (WALMI) in Belur village, on the outskirts of Dharwad city. It was formally inaugurated on 28th August 2016. For the academic year 2016–2017, the institute offered B. Tech courses in three branches, viz. electrical engineering, computer science, and mechanical engineering.

As part of the mentorship plan, IIT Bombay is the mentor institute for IIT Dharwad. The HRD ministry has set up an IIT monitoring cell at IIT Bombay. The committee members were designated as officials on special duty to supervise the process of setting up IIT Dharwad.

The late Union Human Resources Development Minister, S. R. Bommai, had moved the proposal to the Centre seeking an IIT in Dharwad in the 1990s. In 1998, a committee headed by the former ISRO chairman and space scientist, Udupi Ramachandra Rao, submitted its report recommending an IIT in Hubballi-Dharwad. The then Union Finance Minister, Arun Jaitley, in the 2015-16 union budget, sanctioned a budget for an IIT in Karnataka state, and the state government suggested three locations. The shortlisted cities were Dharwad, Mysuru and Raichur.

IIT Dharwad is functioning out of the campus of the Water and Land Management Institute in Dharwad near the Karnataka High Court Bench. A permanent building is coming up at Chikkamaligawad village.

Around 500 acres belonging to KIADB near Mummigatti on the Pune-Bangalore National Highway off Dharwad was identified for the IIT campus, but that deal was cancelled due to legal hurdles. The state cabinet decided to allot 470 acres of land at Kelageri village adjunct to Mammigahtti Industrial Area in Dharwad district. The historic Kittur Fort is 20 kilometres from the campus. The city also houses educational institutions like Karnataka University, Karnatak Science, Arts and Commerce College, University of Agricultural Sciences, SDMCET and Karnataka State Law University. New institutes such as the IIIT Dharwad are coming up in the twin cities of Hubballi-Dharwad. There is also the NTTF tool and die making educational institute at Dharwad.

There is an airport at Gokul Road, Hubballi, the twin city of Dharwad. The airport has air services connecting to Ahmedabad, Bengaluru, Chennai, Hindon-Delhi, Goa, Hyderabad, Kannur, Kochi, Mumbai and Tirupati. There is a railway station at Dharwad through which trains from Bengaluru to Goa run. Hubballi junction is the major railway junction, which has train connections to Kochuveli, Bengaluru, Mumbai, Hyderabad, Varanasi, Howrah, Chennai, Hazrat Nizamuddin, Kolhapur, Solapur, Vijayawada and Vasco, among others. Hubballi city is the headquarters of the southwestern railway zone of Indian Railways.

Departments

- Computer Science and Engineering
- Electrical Engineering

- Mechanical Engineering
- Engineering Physics

IIT Jammu

Indian Institute of Technology Jammu (IIT Jammu) is a public research university located in Jammu, Jammu and Kashmir. As one of India's premier Indian Institutes of Technology, the university came into existence in 2016 when a memorandum of understanding between the Department of Higher Education, Government of Jammu and Kashmir, and the Department of Higher Education, Ministry of Human Resource Development (MHRD), Government of India, was signed. The IIT campus has been constructed in the village of Jagti, in Nagrota Tehsil, in Jammu district.

Set up in the LCD campus, the temporary campus of IIT Jammu has all the facilities required for a hassle-free academic environment—across a total of 40,000 sq. ft. built-up area, housing hostels, house classrooms, a seminar room, a library, a computer laboratory, faculty offices, a cafeteria, and recreational and creative facilities. The campus has volleyball, basketball, badminton courts, and cricket nets. Indoor sports facilities include table tennis, carrom, chess and snooker. Rooms for music, dance and other activities are also available. There is an open-air stage in the academic building, which serves as the centre of cultural activities and performances.

The state government has provided the land, measuring 159 hectares for the establishment of the Indian Institute of Technology at Jammu. The agreement was signed by Prof V. Ramgopal Rao, Director IIT Delhi for and on behalf of MHRD, Government of India (being the mentor institute) and Shri Hemant Sharma, Secretary to Government, Higher Education Department Government of Jammu and Kashmir.

Departments

- Chemical Engineering
- Civil Engineering
- Computer Science and Engineering
- Electrical Engineering
- Materials Engineering
- Mechanical Engineering

IIT Goa

Indian Institute of Technology Goa (IIT Goa) is an autonomous public university located in Goa. An IIT was allotted to Goa by the central government in 2014. The new Indian Institute of Technology in Goa started functioning from July 2016 in a temporary campus housed at Goa Engineering College campus located at Farmagudi, Goa. Currently, it offers B. Tech, M. Tech and PhD courses in various core and one non-core branches, primarily in electrical engineering, computer science and engineering, mechanical engineering, mathematics and computing. It also offers M. Tech and PhD courses.

As part of the mentorship plan, IIT Bombay was the mentor for IIT Goa for three pioneer years. The HRD ministry had set up an IIT monitoring cell at IIT Bombay and the committee members had been designated as officials on special duty to supervise the process of setting up IIT Goa.

The campus is located at Farmagudi, Ponda approximately 29 km southeast of Panaji, the capital of Goa, and it is a temporary campus. The state of Goa is well-connected by roadways, railways and airways with various parts of the country. At present, IIT Goa is temporarily accommodated and functioning at the Goa Engineering College campus located at Farmagudi, Goa. The Goa government had identified land for a permanent campus in Guleli village panchayat in North Goa's Sattari subdistrict, measuring approximately 320 acres. It has been approved by the Union Ministry of Human Resources

Development (HRD). The MHRD expects IIT Goa to function from the temporary campus for the initial three years and it is expected to move to its permanent facility by the fourth year.

Departments

- Computer Science and Engineering
- Electrical Engineering
- Mechanical Engineering

References

Section: "All About the Newer IITs"

Sl. No.	IIT Name	Reference link
1	IIT Kharagpur	https://en.wikipedia.org/wiki/IIT_Kharagpur
2	IIT Bombay	https://en.wikipedia.org/wiki/Indian_Institute_of_Technology_Bombay
3	IIT Madras	https://en.wikipedia.org/wiki/IIT_Madras
4	IIT Kanpur	https://en.wikipedia.org/wiki/Indian_Institute_of_Technology_Kanpur
5	IIT Delhi	https://en.wikipedia.org/wiki/Indian_Institute_of_Technology_Delhi
6	IIT Guwahati	https://en.wikipedia.org/wiki/Indian_Institute_of_Technology_Guwahati
7	IIT Roorkee	https://en.wikipedia.org/wiki/Indian_Institute_of_Technology_Roorkee
8	IIT Ropar	https://en.wikipedia.org/wiki/Indian_Institute_of_Technology_Ropar
9	IIT Bhubaneswar	https://en.wikipedia.org/wiki/Indian_Institute_of_Technology_Bhubaneswar
10	IIT Gandhinagar	https://en.wikipedia.org/wiki/Indian_Institute_of_Technology_Gandhinagar
11	IIT Hyderabad	https://en.wikipedia.org/wiki/IIT_Hyderabad

12	IIT Jodhpur	https://en.wikipedia.org/wiki/Indian_Institute_of_Technology_Jodhpur
13	IIT Patna	https://en.wikipedia.org/wiki/Indian_Institute_of_Technology_Patna
14	IIT Indore	https://en.wikipedia.org/wiki/Indian_Institute_of_Technology_Indore
15	IIT Mandi	https://en.wikipedia.org/wiki/Indian_Institute_of_Technology_Mandi
16	IIT (BHU) Varanasi	https://en.wikipedia.org/wiki/Indian_Institute_of_Technology,_BHU
17	IIT Palakkad	https://en.wikipedia.org/wiki/Indian_Institute_of_Technology_Palakkad
18	IIT Tirupati	https://en.wikipedia.org/wiki/Indian_Institute_of_Technology_Tirupati
19	IIT (ISM) Dhanbad	https://en.wikipedia.org/wiki/Indian_Institute_of_Technology_Dhanbad
20	IIT Bhilai	https://en.wikipedia.org/wiki/Indian_Institute_of_Technology_Bhilai
21	IIT Dharwad	https://en.wikipedia.org/wiki/IIT_Dharwad
22	IIT Jammu	https://en.wikipedia.org/wiki/Indian_Institute_of_Technology_Jammu
23	IIT Goa	https://en.wikipedia.org/wiki/Indian_Institute_of_Technology_Goa

Made in the USA
Monee, IL
17 May 2022

96576827R00148